Faithful Efforts

BRAM DE MUYNCK AND ROEL KUIPER (eds.)

Faithful Efforts

Education, Formation, and the Church

Summum

Cover design: Brainstorm
Typesetting: Gewoon Geertje

ISBN 9789492701343

Copyright © Summum Academic Publications, Kampen, The Netherlands, 2021.
www.summumacademic.com

All rights reserved. No part of this publication may be reproduced, translated, stored in aretrieval system, or transmitted in any form by any means, electronic, mechanical, photocopying, recording or otherwise, without prior written permission from the publisher.

Content

Introduction — 7
Bram de Muynck and Roel Kuiper

1. **Formation: can we trace the influences?** — 13
   Bram de Muynck

2. **"Grace floats in the air." Faith, Formation, and Pedagogical Design** — 23
   David I. Smith

3. **What do we mean by Christian learning? Equipping Christian teachers for their vocation in public education.** — 37
   Trevor Cooling

4. **"So that they won't be like their fathers…" Traditioning and the Theological Limits of the "Formation" Discourse** — 57
   Bernd Wannenwetsch

5. **Formation for Ministry: Dilemmas and Perspectives** — 75
   Hans Schaeffer

6. **Formation in the Church by the 'lex orandi, lex credendi'- Rule (LOLC) from the perspective of Hebrews** — 93
   Maarten Kater

7. **Formation Activities Considered through the Lenses of Attitudes, Cognition and Perception – Elucidation from the Perspective of the Letter to the Hebrews** — 107
   Ferdi Kruger

8. **Teaching Social Animals. The role of the school and the church in civic education** — 131
   Roel Kuiper

Contributors — 143
Index — 145

Introduction

Bram de Muynck and Roel Kuiper

This book brings together selected lectures presented at the *Education, Formation and the Church* conference held in Kampen on 30 and 31 August 2018. The aim of the conference was to provide a platform for academics and professionals to think about formation processes in Christian churches and schools. The urgency of the topic is experienced by many people committed to the faith development of children and young people. Changes in society bring uncertainty and anxiety to churches, schools and families. Some Christian communities are inclined to protect their members from the perceived negative influences of the post-Christian age, while others equip them with tools to become virtuous disciples of Christ in modern society. These all are faithful efforts that seek the best for the future generation. Different responses to the challenges in society affect the various contexts in which formation is at stake, including schools, youth work, catechism and the training of pastors.

During the conference, scholars working in the domains of education and practical theology shared their perspectives, and we discovered that the disciplines have much to learn from each other. This is not surprising, as they have common interests. Believers who promote formation in different contexts belong to the worldwide *ecclesia* of Christ, and the young people they work for also belong or are invited to that ecclesia. This ecclesiastical perspective does not restrict the formation issue to the developmental processes of individuals. According to Paul's epistle to Ephesus, the formation process matters to the church as a whole and therefore has to be seen as a collective phenomenon. Formation takes place for the 'edifying of the body of Christ: till we all come in the unity of the faith, and of the knowledge of the Son of God, unto a perfect man, unto the measure of the fulness of Christ' (Ephesus 4: 12–13). The collective ideal provide the motivation for all the material presented in this book.

We intentionally placed the keyword of the title, *formation*, in its centre because we wanted to stress to focus on the processes that aim to come in the direction of the afore mentioned ideal. Formation towards the fulness of Christ ought to be furthered by such endeavours as education, preaching, catechism, and youth work. We assume that there is much overlap between formation processes in schools and churches and that the ends to which teachers and church leaders strive have a great deal in common. The collective ideal diminishes the significance of adjectives that could be used to precise formation; distinctions are made between spiritual formation, moral formation, personhood formation, identity formation, character formation, and so on, all of which indicate an aspect of the formation process being studied. We do not problematize this variety of terms but use formation as a tentative concept that unites the interests of actors in Churches and schools. The aim of the conference was to create an open context in which participants could reflect using their own terminology. We sometimes speak of formation and sometimes of faith formation. We do not restrict the meaning of formation to the development of young people but also include professional formation in theological seminaries. The last three chapters of this book strongly emphasize the latter.

In the book, when we speak about schools, we mean primary and secondary schools; that is, schools that operate from a Christian foundation, some with strong relationships to the Church and others that are run as independent bodies.

The key issue tackled by all contributors was how we can properly understand formation in the formative contexts of school and Church.

Bram de Muynck (chapter 1) starts with the observation that there are many family, school and Church factors that influence the development of young people. In a context dominated by digital media, the configuration of these domains differs significantly from a few decades ago. He argues that for contemporary faith formation, there is an urgent need to distinguish between the environment and the developing person as the main actor in the formation process. Formation is not the work of a potter but the unique response to stimuli in the environment. Religious educators need to take into account an active hermeneutic space more than before and challenge and feed it with thorough knowledge content, without the pretence of controlling the formation.

Trevor Cooling (chapter 2) provides us with a treatise on the nature of Christian learning. He notices that many teachers feel that they have to impart Christian truths, while their pedagogical intuition tells them that learning is a matter of inquisitive discovery. Cooling shows that this contradiction is unnecessary if one takes a critically realistic position in which one accepts the proper authority of Holy Scripture and realises that learning always requires a hermeneutic that includes personal responsibility. Christian learning thus involves both listening to an authoritative voice and profound hermeneutical competence. Helping teachers to look at learning in this way solves their dilemma without having to give up a conservative faith. At the same time, it encourages students to become wise interpreters.

Similar to Cooling, *David I. Smith* (chapter 3) points out that the transmission of truths floats away from the broad scope of Christian faith. Using four examples, he shows the necessity of paying attention to the pedagogical design of the learning environment. A faith formation curriculum should be regarded as more than just a sequence of topics to be covered; it should consist of a complex environmental design in which all aspects of the environment are considered. The material and symbolic resources and aesthetic and temporal patterns that shape the learning experience should be part of the design.

Berndt Wannenwetsch (chapter 4) approaches faith formation from an entirely different perspective. Starting with Psalm 78, he criticizes current conceptions of formation. He understands formation as a neo-Aristotelian approach to virtue that responds to the dominant liberal paradigm. Due to its strong popularisation, from corporations to theology, formation has acquired a strategic connotation. He presents an alternative paradigm based on Psalm 78, which helps conceptualize formation in a new way. Whereas, in the neo-Aristotelian approach, formation is strongly related to the *polis*, in traditioning, the *torah* is the frame of reference. In the Greek approach, the aim of formation is always the survival of the polis. Virtues are always 'armed'; they help to defend the polis. This is not the case with the Torah, which is the living word that comes from the outside, is always liberating and ensures that the new generation puts its hope in God. Traditioning thus makes room for a liberating discontinuity in which the present generation must expose the new generation to the active power of the living word but does not want to take control of the formation process.

The following three chapters deal with formation as it takes place in the context of training ministers. *Hans Schaeffer* (chapter 5) addresses the need for formation in the education of future ministers within Christian communities because of the disbalance he perceives between knowledge, theological reflection and spiritual formation. He explains how three dilemmas in theological education are at stake: whether spiritual formation is manageable; to what degree embeddedness in church practices and academic reflection are contradictory; and whether theology is about content or method. This article opens up a new way of thinking through formation for ministry from the angle of liturgical formation as a possible way to deal with the three dilemmas noted.

Maarten Kater (chapter 6) discusses the background of the expression *lex orandi, lex credendi* and the importance of a proper understanding of it in theological education. Beyond its meaning, the linguistic and historical connotations of this Latin phrase suggest that how you pray reveals what you believe. The expression is sometimes interpreted as a normative sequence in the formation of doctrine. The doctrine reflects church practices. The author's interpretation of the Letter to the Hebrews shows that this stance is problematic. What one believes can potentially correct liturgical practices. It is interesting how the theme relates to the formation of individuals and groups through the evaluation of habits, rituals and liturgies, which are at the centre of reflections on how people worship (think of the work of James K Smith, also referred to in chapters 1, 2, 5 and 8).

Ferdi Kruger's contribution (chapter 7) also deals with the formation of students at theological institutions, but unlike Kater, instead of Church history, he consults educational science. He attempts to use the concepts of attitude, cognition and perception to provide insights into how formation processes work. He places these educational views against the background of new developments in education, which can be placed under the heading 'transformative education', and uses psychological insights from Piaget and Vygotsky. Piaget, for example, emphasised that, based on their experiences, learners constantly reorganise their existing cognitive schemas. Teachers are wise to actively engage students in education to enable them to make adjustments to their schemas.

Roel Kuiper (chapter 8) discusses a new perspective: formation as socialization. Preparing students for their role in society is a felt obligation for schools and also for churches. Since we are members of society we need social education. Christian schools have seen this as part of their biblical teaching about the 'cultural mandate'. Herman Bavinck once remarked that 'justice and love are of more worth for society than knowledge'. Active citizenship should not be far away from the curriculum of Christian schools. Civic attitudes, however, are formed in and through practices. Schools can relate their educational approach to practices that serve the common good. In this process personal values and good behavior are stimulated. Schools need to create a shared repertoire of ideas, concepts, routines, stories, symbols, actions to train their students. Moral and cultural formation will help them to see their public role and serve in the world out there.

We are grateful to *Stichting Afbouw,* related to Theological University Kampen and *Stichting Horizon,* related to the theological University of Apeldoorn, for their generous contributions to the cost of this publication. We also thank Wenneke de Ruijter for her editorial support. We hope that the articles of this book support and strengthen in their own way the faithful efforts of educators in schools and churches. We also hope that researchers in academia will find insights in the book that will be fruitful for their work.

1. Formation: can we trace the influences?

Bram de Muynck

Introduction

The great Dutch educationalist P. A. Kohnstamm (1865-1951) was of the opinion that personal formation is an ongoing process. The formation of personhood starts at birth and ends when a person has died.[1] The only thing that counts in this process is whether one reaches inner peace. Kohnstamm was also of the opinion that all formation is self-formation. It is not the environment that forms the person, but it is the person that forms himself.[2] This raises the question about the surrounding people who intend to have a positive influence on the development of a person; specifically parents, teachers and youth workers, who have a certain idea regarding this development, even, perhaps, a religious ideal. I think especially of course about those who are touched themselves by the liberating message of the gospel and desire this experience also for the developing person. An urgent issue, in the context of Christian families, church congregations and Christian schools, is that many young people apparently do not arrive at the conscious moment of affirmation of faith that their parents and Church educators wish for them. Yearbooks of the churches in the Netherlands testify to decreasing numbers of young people openly confessing their faith during confirmation ceremonials. Statistics on reformed denominations report a decrease of 25% in this regard and also report a significant difference between baptised and confirmed children. Another issue that makes formation a subject for reflection is the enormous impact of social media. They influence children and young people in such a way that regular educators have little grip on them. In this article, I will address the question who the people of influence are in the formation of young people and how the furthering of the formation process must be understood. First, I will examine what is meant by formation. I will do this with the question in mind whether and

---

[1] Philip Abraham Kohnstamm, *Persoonlijkheid in wording. Schets ener Christelijke opvoedkunde.* (Haarlem: H.D. Tjeenk Willink & Zoon N.V., 1959), 10–12.
[2] Kohnstamm, *Persoonlijkheid*, 137.

how influences can be traced; other authors in this volume will critically reflect on formation from other perspectives. Then, I will examine the position of educators in the various institutions in which children and young people participate. In doing so, I will distinguish between context, climate and intervention. I will conclude with some remarks about the interrelated tasks of school and church educators. I begin by presenting a case study, to which I will return over the course of the argument.

George
George is a young adult I interviewed as part of a research project I was conducting.[3] George, who was still studying at university, told me a lot of details his spiritual biography. He said that he would call himself a believing Christian since his second year of studying mathematics. When asked whether this conscious experience of faith was self-sustaining, he told me that his childhood experiences were important, but as such they were not a positive precursor of the development of his faith, and how this development precisely occurred, was unclear to him. His parents were devoted church members, read bible stories when he was young, sent him to a Christian school but hardly talked about faith. God was mentioned only when the children had done something seriously wrong. A warning would follow: 'God in heaven is observing us'. As a child, he often felt afraid of God and of the threat of ordeal. Some positive messages he received from a teacher when he was in the eighth grade; someone who was speaking with deep respect and intensely warm love about the Lord. After a period of disinterest in early adolescence, he began to think about the role of God in his life. He started to read the Bible and to pray again, which led him to a conscious affirmation of God's promises for his life. He said to be thankful for all the knowledge he acquired as a child. George told me, however, that his development could also have turned into a decision not to believe. He experiences faith as a miracle that cannot be attributed to a single event evoked by a sermon.

Formation
I consider the kind of faith formation that I was inquiring in this interview as a part of the formation of personhood.[4] It can even be regarded as the core of education, because religious attitudes, values and convictions influence every other area of life. For example, religious formation is

---
3 Research project into the role of covenant in formation processes. Report in progress.
4 Bram de Muynck, *Tijd voor verlangen* (Apeldoorn: TUA, 2016).

linked to social interaction with peers as well as the way one views one's own social and cultural environment. Religious education has a contemplative or spiritual aspect (one is brought up with the desire to become a God-fearing person); a moral aspect (one is initiated into the precepts that flow directly from faith, also called discipleship); a social-emotional aspect (one is guided on the road to stable maturity); but also a cognitive aspect (one is introduced to knowledge about the Bible, religious doctrine and beliefs about culture and society). The latter aspect is often strongly emphasised in religious education. Religious education is experienced as synonymous with education in the church or the subject of classes in religion at school. It is not by chance that the concept of formation overlaps considerably with ideas concerning education. The concept of formation also has other connotations, such as imitation, training, being shaped like a pot by the potter.

In continental philosophy, however, the concept of formation has connotations that need not be linked directly to education. The German term *Bildung* refers to the process of allowing oneself to be nourished by the intellectual, spiritual and aesthetic sources of cultural history; according to the Bildung tradition, a good education embodies some of these. If one is well formed, one can be self-reflective, can look at oneself from a distance. Well-trained young people can also distance themselves from the craving for immediate gratification.[5] Another effect of *Bildung* is that people with a rich mental baggage arrive at independent judgements. They know how to evaluate all the information they take in. When it comes to Christian formation, one will be able and willing to connect what is of value from the Christian tradition in the footsteps of Jesus Christ. In this tradition, formation does not coincide seamlessly with culture and civilisation, but, can, in fact, come into conflict with them. Dietrich Bonhoeffer (1906-1944) spoke critically of all too superficial ideas of formation and believed that Christian formation means that one becomes more and more like the figure of Christ as a person: the incarnate, the crucified, the risen, and that this is why Christian formation withdraws itself from planning and programmes.[6] The imagery that Bonhoeffer's uses has strong roots in the Gospels, for example in Jesus' words about

---

5 Bram de Muynck and Pieter Vos, "Geen vorming zonder transcendentie. De theologische horizon van een breed pedagogisch vormingsbegrip" in *Mens worden. Over de relatie tussen Theologie en pedagogiek*, ed. Wolter Huttinga and Roel Kuiper (Amsterdam: Buijten & Schipperheijn, 2021), 151-170.
6 Dietrich Bonhoeffer, *Ethik* (München: Chr. Kaiser Verlag, 1966), 85.

the yoke in Matt. 11: 28-30: 'Come to me, all you who are weary and burdened, and I will give you rest. Take my yoke upon you and learn from me, for I am gentle and humble in heart, and you will find rest for your souls. For my yoke is easy and my burden is light' (Matth. 11:27-28, NIV). The image is that of a yoke that is laid upon two animals. The two are forced to walk together in the same pace. When Jesus applies the image to his disciples, he invites them to unite with him. The disciples bear the yoke, not alone but together with Jesus. The message behind this is that of the unity of master and learner, of the learner with the master; not so much of training or imitation. Biblical talk of education shows that pedagogy and theology do not naturally harmonise in their deeper meaning. The Christian reflection on formation is challenged by this tension, which we will see in other contributions in this volume.

Actors in formation: who has the key?
Involved actors in formation, like parents, teachers and youth workers will always have their influence in the process of education and formation. They cannot not act, something happens anyway. When one values faith, one always will communicate more or less certain content or attitudes regarding that faith. This was also the case with George's parents. They were devoted believers and tried to communicate something about their faith to the best of their abilities. Even if the effect was not what they had hoped for, something was communicated. This raises the question of how the influencing person relates to the influenced person. Is it George who forms himself, or is he formed by his parents and the teacher who made such an impression on him?

Formation is sometimes taken to mean 'being pressed into a mould'; for example, using the image of a potter. Forming something is then equivalent to working towards a copy of an already existing model. This image is usually viewed negatively by the Western educational ideal.[7] It is associated with drilling and conditioning rather than with making people curious and developing talent. A potter forms a piece according to a certain predefined format. It must become exactly as he had imagined it, without the object he makes having any influence on its ideal form. In a narrower sense, we can also say that formation is done by working towards a general idea. This is often also the case with artists. They have a general image in mind and they gradually work towards it. The beauty unfolds while the artist is working. Something similar can be said of

---

7 Bram de Muynck and Pieter Vos, *Geen vorming*, 153.

educators. Whomever they are —parents, teachers or youth workers, they will always be more or less unconscious carriers of ideals. The object of formation, however, does not behave like an object, but as a subject. If we were to stay with the metaphor of the potter, the subject at least gives resistance, just as material gives resistance. So there is a mutual influence, reciprocity. Because the formed object resists on the basis of certain properties, the forming actor adapts.[8] This aligns with the general view of most educators: their influence is limited. They will inspire, encourage and provide stimulation, but do not want the person to become a copy of themselves.

The complicated thing about formation is that each person goes his particular way.[9] The person is exposed to many influences, but ultimately decides on the direction of his life. From a Christian anthropological point of view, we can say that the person can do this as a result of his own hermeneutical space.[10] Therefore it is correct to say, with Kohnstamm, that all education is self-formation. This point of view is also illustrated in other contributions to this volume. A person is educated to take more and more personal responsibility and to live independently in the service of God and of his neighbours.[11] This does not mean that the person makes autonomous decisions from an early age; this is impossible. Educators are provided to take responsibility for the child, at least temporarily. Educators act proactively: they do not let the child go its own way in a free space, but anticipate increasing responsibility. Therefore, they guide the child in such a way that it is given room to explore and is pointed in the right direction. In this way, they promote the child's ability to make its own commitments. In light of all these considerations, we define formation as the ongoing interaction of influences on the person (deliberate and not deliberate) and the unique processing of those influences by the person.[12]

---

8   Bram de Muynck en Pieter Vos, *Geen vorming*, 154-155.
9   Anne-Marije de Bruin-Wassinkmaat, *Finding one's own way: Exploring the religious identity development of emerging adults raised in strictly Reformed contexts in the Netherlands*. PhD dissertation (Amsterdam, Protestant Theological University, 2021).
10 Didier Pollefeyt, "Religious education as opening the hermeneutical space," Journal of Religious Education 68 (2020): 115–124, doi.org/10.1007/s40839-020-00105-7.
11 Bram de Muynck and Elsbeth Visser-Vogel, "A Christian perspective on personhood formation: theological premises in dialogue with theoretical frameworks," *Journal of Research on Christian Education* 29, no. 2 (2020): 105–125. DOI: 10.1080/10656219.2020.1767010
12 Compare Bram de Muynck and Elsbeth Visser-Vogel, "A Christian perspective".

Context, climate and interventions

Formation is thus a mutual process in which the forming person must be seen as the most important actor. At the same time, educators are fully responsible for how they act in their relation to the forming person. To elucidate their responsibilities, I distinguish between formational context, formational climate and formational interventions.[13] The context refers to the domain in which influence is exercised; for example, the family, the church or the school. The climate reflects the everyday interactions that take place in that context, and the interventions are the actions of the educators by which he arranges his or her influence. I will explain these concepts in more detail.

Formational context

Formational contexts include the formal institutions of family, church and school, as well as less formal influences such as sports clubs, groups of friends and social media. For the sake of clarity, I have left broader socio-historical and cultural contexts out of consideration, not because they are not important in themselves, but because, in the present contribution, I am mainly looking for the relative significance of various actors in the formation process.

The significance of the various formal institutions seems to be shifting. Networks of young people are becoming more important and networks of parents are also becoming more important.[14] Amidst these shifts, the family seems to retain its significance as the primary influential context. Formal institutions, like school and church, seem to have a more secondary or additional role in formation. This has to do not only with the fact that parents are usually present at the beginning of the formation process, but also that they are irreplaceable. In all other institutions, actors are passers-by (teachers, pastors, youth workers); parents are not. Parents are legally responsible for their children. Religious parents, moreover, are bound by a transcendent obligation to raise their children in a religious manner. There is the claim that salvation is not only for the

---

13 Bram de Muynck and Bram Kunz, *Gidsen. Een christelijke schoolpedagogiek.* (Utrecht: KokBoekencentrum, 2021), pp. 180–182.
14 Daniëlle van Koot-Dees, *Prille geloofsopvoeding. Een kwalitatief onderzoek naar de rol van geloven in jonge protestants-christelijke gezinnen in Amsterdam* (Zoetermeer: Boekencentrum Academic, 2013), 350–354; Hans van Crombrugge, "Moeten we de schotten tussen school, gezin en parochie ophalen?" in *Tegen-woordig. Jeugd en geloofscummunicatie vandaag*, ed. Didier Pollefeyt and Ellen De Boeck (Leuven/Den Haag: Acco, 2012), 113–133.

present generation but also for the coming one. Parents raise their children religiously based on the conviction that they are included in the covenant (from a reformed perspective) or that they are, at least, blessed in the circle of the faithful (from an anabaptist perspective). Studies conducted in recent decades consistently show that the family is the most important socialising environment, also in terms of religious development. These studies are similar in their low prioritisation of the school for this development.[15] This does not mean, however, that actors within these contexts cannot be important. George, for example, mainly attributed an important influence to one teacher. Research also shows that actors in environments other than the family play a compensating role.[16] In the various contexts, however, we can discern emphasizes in the intended and experienced influence.

While church actors (the pastor, the youth worker) focus mainly on spiritual phenomena, the family (parents and important others) primarily addresses socio-emotional phenomena, and the school (teachers) primarily addresses cognitive phenomena. It is important that not only the formal bearers of a role can have an influence, but also those who play an important role in the same context. This includes, for example, classmates at school with whom one is friends, the sexton at church who greets everyone warmly, or the friends of one's parents, who are always interested in the child.

Formational climate
The formational climate represents what the person experiences in everyday life in a specific context. It involves everyday speech, interaction, atmosphere, social dynamics. It always concerns a combination of actors and factors in the environment. As far as the actors are concerned (for example the parent, the teacher, the youth worker), the way in which they present themselves physically from moment to moment is important. The forming person reads meanings from, for example, gestures, facial expressions and tone of voice, and internalises them to a greater or lesser

---

15 Joep de Hart, *Levensbeschouwelijke en politieke praktijken van Nederlandse middelbare scholieren* (Kampen: Kok, 1990); Hans Alma, *Geloven in de leefwereld van jongeren* (Kampen: Kok, 1993); S. Fisherman, "Socialization Agents Influencing the Religious Identity of Religious Israeli Adolescents," *Religious Education* 106, no. 3 (2011): 272–298, DOI: 10.1080/00344087.2011.569653.

16 Simone de Roos, "Young Children's God Concepts: Influences of Attachment and Religious Socialization in a Family and School Context," *Religious Education* 101, no. 1 (2006): 84–103.

extent. That is what George identifies in the behaviour of his teacher. The words spoken 'with deep respect and with intensely warm love about the Lord' were observed as something significant. The tone seems to have communicated something that touched his heart. Together with other factors in the environment (such as the orderliness or messiness of the house, the decorations on the wall or the furnishings of a classroom), the child's actions are perceived as part of the climate. German research has shown that a positive classroom climate is a favourable precondition for religious development.[17] A complex of actions and characteristics of the environment make a pupil feel love, trust and security. This is what can also be called implicit pedagogy, which will be an important issue in this book. James K. Smith's studies on cultural liturgies demonstrate how the environment shapes the person. Rituals, habits and liturgies in the environment shape the person's habitus, 'that nexus of dispositions by which we constitute our world without rational deliberation or conscious awareness'.[18] Habitus is an acquired second nature that is neither natural nor instinctive, neither conscious nor deliberative.[19] In Smith's conception, the influence of rituals, customs and liturgies is important because all manner of these intermingle. A developing person is not only engaged in the liturgies of family life (e.g. daily prayers), school life (e.g. hearing Bible stories), or congregational gatherings (containing a variety of liturgical elements), but also in those of the surrounding world, such as shopping on the weekend, sharing pictures on Instagram or Facebook, and so on.

Formational interventions
Thirdly, there are the formative interventions that are intended to influence the individual. These can be programmes that are primarily concerned with cognitive development, as in the aforementioned education or catechesis in the church and the religious curriculum at school. David I. Smith, in his contribution in this volume, will extensively explain why a careful design of a curriculum is important. However, there is also a category of interventions that is much more incidental and that appears

---

17 E. Hennecke, *Was lernen Kinder im Religionsunterricht? Eine fallbezogene und thematische Analyse kindlicher Rezeptionen von Religionsunterricht.* (Dissertatie, Fakultät für Geisteswissenschaften Institut für Katholische Theologie der Universität Duisburg-Essen, 2011).
18 James K. Smith, *Desiring the Kingdom* (Grand Rapids: Baker Academic, 2013), 82.
19 Smith, *Desiring,* 83

suddenly in everyday life. In George's case, this is exemplified by those moments in which he had done something wrong. God was mentioned at that moment, which evoked in George the anxiety of God. This pedagogical intervention arises in the bedding of the pedagogical everyday life. A certain moment in the relationship forces the educator to make a decision in the interest of the pupil. That decision can be anything, varying from asking a question, making a correction, having an individual conversation, singing a song together, reading a story, or praying for something together. Therefore, there is potential that the educator uses in the pedagogical climate of everyday life. Different competences to intervene are usually attributed to influencers dependent of the context they operate in. If one works in a school or is educated as a youth worker, one has received training in conscious intervention. Parents have to make it with their intuition, what they have seen as examples and what they have learned through experience. If formation, however, is seen as a collective event, as happens in a Christian view (see the introduction), then the untrained educator is not alone. There are brothers and sisters who can advise and assist the educator.

Concluding remarks
In this contribution, I have explored the influences that play a role in the process of formation. I have distinguished among the various contexts in which children and young people are influenced, the climate that characterises everyday interaction in each of these contexts and the pedagogical interventions that the various actors in these contexts deliberately use. In terms of contexts, the family appears to be the most important. This is the most fundamental context, of course, for someone's upbringing. If other actors have a greater influence, they appear mainly to be compensating for what is missing from the family. When we look at the whole from a distance, it does not seem that the systematically deployed programmes are the most influential. In biographical reflections, it is the relationships with specific people, that appear to have significant impact. In the case of George, it is the teacher, that apparently was the most important actor in his faith formation. This indicates that significant formative influences are difficult to steer and control. They come about in certain contexts where the child or adolescent assigns meaning. For outsiders, the formation is only partly perceptible, but also for the key actor, the person self. What forms him or her and what exactly is formed is a secret that can only be reconstructed in retrospect. This is not merely an empirical fact, and thus capable of being called a mystery beyond

control.[20] It also fits with how the Gospel speaks of faith: 'The wind blows wherever it pleases. You hear its sound, but you cannot tell where it comes from or where it is going. So it is with everyone born of the Spirit' (John 3:8). This is not to say that systematic (curricular) interventions should not matter. They function, at least, as a source of meaning, a source that helps to interpret reality and direct someone's attention. In the interview, George did not talk about the way he absorbed religion lessons or heard sermons. At the same time, it is clear from what he said that the religious vocabulary has helped him to interpret the meaning of faith. This made him thankful for the stories he heard and the knowledge about God. This affirms Kohnstamm's view that formation is in the end self-formation. This shows also why actors should not neglect the programmatic, but at the same time be aware of its relative meaning and pay attention to the competence to act pedagogically with wisdom and to be authentically present in all contexts.[21] The following two chapters will concentrate on teaching and learning in the school context. Chapter 4 leads us to formational practices in the Church context. The next three chapters deal with the context of theology education, and the final chapter broadens the perspective to the school again, in its wider social context.

---

20 Bram de Muynck and Elsbeth Visser, *A Christian Perspective*, 111.
21 Hans van Crombrugge, *Schotten*, 128

2. "Grace floats in the air."
Faith, Formation, and Pedagogical Design

David I. Smith

Introduction: Formation and Floating Faith

In one suggestive formulation of Abraham Kuyper's well-known protest against the modern tendency toward separation of faith from the wider processes of social life he warns that all too often "particular grace floats in the air"[1]. The phrase evokes a modern tendency for beliefs about salvation to become unmoored from the broader workings of the world. Particular grace then seems to address the religious parts of life, while the rest of life remains under the sway of other ideological accents. It then becomes relatively easy to confess Christian faith while, say, voting according to the interests of our ethnic group or wallet, consuming as avidly as the average person, or embracing an individualistic and materialistic definition of professional success. If particular grace "floats in the air," it becomes a kind of hot air balloon: decorative, evocative of peace and transcendence, perhaps even impressive and majestic, but not something we use to actually travel to the office or bring home the groceries.

Kuyper complained that modern Christians easily end up living in "two spheres of thought." These are "On the one hand, the very narrow, reduced line of thought involving your soul's salvation, and on the other hand the broad, spacious, life-encompassing sphere of thought involving the world. Your Christ then belongs comfortably in that first, reduced sphere of thinking, but not in the broad one"[2]. Yet this formulation itself risks another kind of floating. We do not simply live in, nor are we necessarily primarily shaped by "spheres of thought," as if our troubles could be solved simply by thinking more clearly. We are embedded in our material and social environments. We are shaped by our dreams, desires, and loves, which are rooted not just in intellectual frameworks, but in a

---

1 Craig G. Bartholomew, *Contours of the Kuyperian Tradition: A Systematic Introduction* (Downers Grove: IVP Academic, 2017), 39.
2 Bartholomew, *Contours,* 39.

more basic, bodily response to the world[3]. A faith focused too doggedly on getting the thinking part right may still float free from the realm of embodied practices and the dispositions they shape[4].

The language of "faith formation" and its increased popularity in the context of theological education[5] implies something more than instruction in belief. Recent literature on "faith formation," "spiritual formation," or "Christian formation" commonly draws a contrast with mere information[6]. It implies a whole self being shaped as it moves through the world and grows into a calling. Yet even here the risk of floating remains. If "faith" itself is imagined as a thing that inhabits a separate, religious realm, then "faith formation" may still be about building better hot air balloons. In practical terms, "faith formation" may end up mainly associated with the religion class, chapel program, or prayer meetings, or with specific focal interventions such as spiritual practices, service projects, or personal mentoring[7]. All of this may leave relatively untouched the pedagogical decisions that shape everyday teaching and learning[8].

Yet if formation happens, at least in part, in response to the practices that make up teaching and learning, then the relationship between teaching and faith formation is not restricted to the moments when faith or spirituality are explicitly in focus. Astley suggests that "formation" denotes "all the processes of teaching and/or learning that help to shape a learner in a tradition and its beliefs, experiences and practices, in a way

---

3 James K. A. Smith, *Desiring the Kingdom: Worship, Worldview, and Cultural Formation* (Grand Rapids: Baker Academic, 2009); Robert Sweetman, *Tracing the Lines: Spiritual Exercise and the Gesture of Christian Scholarship*, (Eugene: Wipf & Stock, 2016).

4 David I. Smith and James K. A. Smith, *Teaching and Christian Practices: Reshaping Faith and Learning* (Grand Rapids: Eerdmans, 2011); Matthew Kaemingk, *Christian Hospitality and Muslim Immigration in an Age of Fear* (Grand Rapids: Eerdmans, 2018).

5 Aaron J. Ghiloni, Is Formation Education? *Journal of Christian Education* 54 (3) (2011):29-41. doi:10.1177/002196571105400305

6 Fred Glennon, et al, "Formation in the Classroom," *Teaching Theology & Religion* 14 (2011): 357-381. doi:10.1111/j.1467-9647.2011.00740.x; Matthew R. Miller and JohnMark Bennett Beazley, "Christian Spiritual Formation in the Classical School," *Journal of Spiritual Formation and Soul Care* 11 (2018): 230-240. doi:10.1177/1939790918796834

7 Paul Bramer, "Introduction to the Special Focus: Spiritual Formation and Christian Education," *Christian Education Journal* 7 (2010): 334–339. doi: 10.1177/073989131000700206; Anne Puidk Horan, "Fostering Spiritual Formation of Millennials in Christian Schools," *Journal of Research on Christian Education* 26 (2017): 56-77. doi:10.1080/10656219.2017.1282901

8 Richard Ramsey, "The Ministry of … Grading?," *Christian Education Journal* 9 (2012): 408-419. doi:10.1177/073989131200900212

that leads to the learner's acceptance of that tradition in her thinking, valuing, feeling and perceiving, and her dispositions to act and experience, together with her appraisal of the tradition's merits and faults"[9]. If "all the processes of teaching and/or learning that help" are relevant, then faith formation and teaching may intersect at points other than overt spiritual practices or theological learning, "even in the most un-subjective, information-filled, and theory-driven classes we teach"[10]. Not just by mentioning theology, but in their overall pedagogical design, teachers may "create classroom conditions that help to shape the hearts and lives of the students in ways that do not hinder the receiving of grace but instead make it easier to believe"[11].

The next problem is that it is not necessarily particularly helpful to be told that everything is relevant. Such an assertion broadens the landscape but provides no specific focus for our attention or action. In this essay, then, I aim to outline some specific connections faith formation and the design of teaching and learning processes. I am less interested in the moments when we are teaching directly about faith, and more interested in what is implied by how we teach[12]. I will proceed largely by way of commenting on concrete examples of teaching and learning. First, however, I will outline a framework that may be useful for understanding those examples.

Complex Environmental Design

Part way through a recent graduate class on curriculum theory, one teacher commented ruefully that he had always tended to think that curriculum was what used to be kept in a row of ring binders in the school office. His comment reflects a common temptation to think of curriculum as basically a sequence of topics to be covered. This conception masks many of the formative ways in which curriculum frames learning when

---

9   Jeff Astley, "The Naming of Parts: Faith, Formation, Development and Education," *Christian Faith, Formation and Education*. Eds. Ros Stuart-Buttle and John Shortt. Cham: Springer Nature, 2008: 22.
10 Fred Glennon, et al, "Formation in the Classroom," 366.
11 Niel Holm, "Classroom Formation & Spiritual Awareness Pedagogy Based on Bonhoeffer's Life Together," *Journal of Education & Christian Belief* 12 (2008): 161. doi: 10.1177/2F205699710801200207.
12 Trevor Cooling and Elizabeth H. Green, "Competing Imaginations for Teaching and Learning: The Findings of Research into a Christian Approach to Teaching and Learning Called What If Learning," *International Journal of Christianity and Education* 19 (2015): 96–107. doi:10.1177/2F2056997115583432.

understood as a set of practices unfolding within a complex environment. Definitions of curriculum are notoriously abundant. For present purposes, I will lean on a six-faceted characterization of curriculum as a process of complex environmental design outlined by Wayne Au[13]. I do not suggest that this is a complete or ultimate account of curriculum (there are other ways to divide up the world). I aim simply to use it to explore some ways in which curricular design might interact with faith formation. Au's model has the significant merit of steering us away from the sense that faith intersects with curriculum mainly as an occasional topic.

Au characterizes curriculum as emerging from a complex design process that interacts with particular social and pedagogical environments[14]. As a learning sequence emerges, it shapes six facets of the learner's environment:

- *Physical materials*, such as furniture, room layout, books, white boards, etc, are chosen and arranged in ways that channel attention and interaction.
- Language and other *symbol systems* (e.g., the images used, the names of chapters, how goals or behaviors are named, gestures, intonation, etc.) shape the meanings we glean from the learning setting.
- Learners engage in a constrained set of *behaviors* (they might, for instance, work alone or in pairs or small groups, pursue individual questions or answer prescribed ones, sit quietly or move round, stay in the classroom or reach beyond it).
- All of this is framed by a particular structuring of *time* (an implied story about past and future that frames the present moment, and a flow of time in which certain things move quickly or slowly, are given more time or less, stand as beginnings or endings).
- The learning process has *aesthetic* qualities, not only through sights and sounds (particular learning resources may be attractive, ugly, anodyne, provocative) but through its particular flow (it might seem tightly sequenced or disconnected, serene or harried).

---

13 Wayne Au, *Critical Curriculum Studies: Education, Consciousness and the Politics of Knowing* (New York: Routledge, 2011); Dwayne E. Huebner, "Curriculum as Concern for Man's Temporality," *The Lure of the Transcendent: Collected Essays by Dwayne E. Huebner*. Ed. Vikki Hillis. Mahwah: Lawrence Erlbaum Associates, 1999: 131-142.
14 Wayne Au, *Critical Curriculum Studies* (New York: Routledge, 2011).

- Finally, everything is influenced by the exercise of *power*, in which some determine for others which stories will be told and silenced, which expressions of self will be accepted as normative, which choices are enacted, and whose voices are audible.

These are not six steps, happening one after the other. They are a simultaneous matrix. All six will interact in any realized design, whether carefully crafted or blundered into thoughtlessly. Learning takes shape within a patterned complex of physical, symbolic, and behavioral affordances and configurations of time, aesthetics, and power.

To make matters more concrete, I propose in what follows to consider four examples of learning taking place in school contexts. I have examined each of these elsewhere in different contexts. Here I bring them together as examples of how the complex design of learning practices may interact with faith formation.

Narrative 1: Grades, theology, and rigor

I begin with an incident drawn from an email communication with one of my former students. The student in question had recently completed his undergraduate studies and had gone on to graduate study in theology at a well-respected seminary. He wrote to me describing his experiences in one of his graduate theology classes:

> In a class on Anglo-American postmodernity I've been frustrated by how assignments are designed. We recently received our first paper back, and I was surprised and somewhat amused to find that almost all of the best students (i.e. those who have taken the most interest in the material, who have asked the most insightful questions, and whom I would just generally like to sit down and have a long talk with about the material) got rather crummy grades. Of about five of the students I have talked to, all students who I see as brighter than myself and who I would like to have look over my work, only one did well while several did miserably. After talking with different people, I've come to suspect that the reason is these students were not content to simply regurgitate information. We realized that what the professor and TA want is basically a boat-load of citations to answer the relatively simple questions. I've been somewhat amused by the result of this, because it has made the last first and the first last—normally C students got mostly A's, while the normally A students got C's. But it is also frustrating, because the path of least resistance to an A is intellectual mediocrity. We all laughed at ourselves because we spent hours on a paper that was really an easy A to get B's and C's.

> What this does, however, is incentivize acquiescence and intellectual apathy. I've run into this now in a few classes, and am beginning to worry that I will not survive seminary with a shred of intellectual rigor left in me[15].

The student describes a learning experience that nurtures a concern that theological study and intellectual rigor might not fit together. I take this to be an instance of faith (mis)formation. The student's relationship to, understanding of, and experience of faith is being influenced, albeit not constructively. The narrative does not suggest that the student has necessarily reached a general conclusion about the nature of faith, rather than about the quality of instruction. However, his worry sits at the intersection of education and his personal sense of how theology sits in the world.

The worry was not generated through the theological positions presented by the instructor. The narrative offers no grounds for making judgements about the instructor's theological acumen or orthodoxy. Nor are we given much insight into the adequacy of the specific assignments used, or the spiritual practices that might have surrounded them. Instead, we glimpse some interactions in the complex environment of learning. Specific material and symbolic resources are in play (papers, assignments, citation conventions, library resources, letters inscribed on student work or in online grade books as symbols of success and approval, the remembered rhetoric of Matthew 19:30). These help to foster behaviors (comparing grades, discussing apparent anomalies, adjusting learning strategies to fit the implied criteria for success). This unfolds as a temporal arc. the grade assigned to the first paper of the semester reveals what seems to be required for success and so nudges learners in a particular direction. The impact on the student's aesthetic experience of the course can be glimpsed in words such as "boatload," "acquiescence," and "apathy." Such language suggests a learning environment associated with dull quantity and needless passivity. The whole process is influenced by the power exercised by the professor and TAs, who design assignments, confer grades and approval, and so set the criteria for success. Their use of this power enhances the success of a selective subset of students while tending to alienate others, even if they were initially highly motivated. All of these facets act together to shape the formative charge of the learning sequence.

---

15 David I. Smith, *On Christian Teaching: Practicing Faith in the Classroom* (Grand Rapids, Eerdmans, 2018), 7-8.

It seems very likely that these processes were not quite those intended or desired by the instructor. Given the avowed mission of the seminary in question, supportive faith formation and constructive student engagement were probably conscious goals. The moves described in the email likely derive less from those goals than from the professor's general socialization into unquestioned classroom practices. In this instance, formation in faith and the formative tug of teaching and learning practices appear to be traveling in different directions.

Narrative 2: Intentional practices
A second, more hopeful example is drawn from student responses to a special topics course on Bonhoeffer during an undergraduate German program at a Christian liberal arts college. I designed the course around Bonhoeffer's text *Gemeinsames Leben*, known in English as *Life Together*[16]. As detailed elsewhere, the process of preparing to teach the course brought to light the lack of resources for learning from Bonhoeffer's text that honor its emphasis on intentional practices rather than treating it primarily as a source of theological ideas[17]. The course that emerged included the usual reading, writing, and discussion assignments, but was also built around a series of practices intended to offer "legitimate, peripheral participation" in Bonhoeffer's design for an intentional Christian learning community[18].

The first assigned practice emerged from reflection on how students might be helped to engage with Bonhoeffer's statement that "our community with one another consists solely in what Christ has done to both of us." Christian community, Bonhoeffer points out, cannot be grounded on whether we enjoy one another's company, ethnicity, or

---

16 Dietrich Bonhoeffer, *Gemeinsames Leben* (Gütersloh: Gütersloher Verlagshaus, 1987); Dietrich Bonhoeffer, "Dietrich Bonhoeffer, Life Together and Prayer Book of the Bible, Dietrich Bonhoeffer Works, Volume 5.," *Dietrich Bonhoeffer Works, Volume 5*. Translated by Daniel W. Bloesch and James H. Burtness. Minneapolis: Fortress Press, 1996.

17 David I. Smith, "Teaching Bonhoeffer: Pedagogy and Peripheral Practices," *International Journal of Christianity and Education* 21 (2017): 146-59. doi: 10.1177/2F20569 97117700430; Craig Dykstra, *Growing in the Life of Faith: Education and Christian Practices*, (Louisville: Westminster John Knox Press, 2005); Stanley Hauerwas, *Performing the Faith: Bonhoeffer and the Practice of Non-Violence* (Grand Rapids: Brazos Press, 2004); Niel Holm, "Classroom Formation & Spiritual Awareness Pedagogy Based on Bonhoeffer's Life Together," *Journal of Education & Christian Belief* 12 (2008): 159-175. doi:10.1177/2F205699710801200207.

18 Jean Lave and Etienne Wenger, *Situated Learning: Legitimate Peripheral Participation* (Cambridge: Cambridge University Press, 1991).

tastes; "we belong to one another only through and in Jesus Christ"[19]. Alongside their reading and journaling tasks, I asked students to choose a person whom they saw most days in the week. If possible, it should be a person with whom they would not choose to spend time. The task was simply to pause each time they saw that person, reflect that they had been accepted by Christ, and offer thanks for their life. After a week of this, one student wrote[20]:

> There's a student with whom I'm not on friendly terms. We don't fight, but when we are together, it can be a bit awkward. Over the course of the last few days I've prayed for this student. The more I prayed for him, the more I found I could stand him. Now I don't find it a problem seeing him around campus. We are not best friends, but I believe that things have improved between us.

During the following week the practice was changed slightly; this time students were asked to pray daily for a person in their environment whose name they did not know. A student reported[21]:

> I learned that it is a humbling experience to pray for someone you don't know. I have to be totally selfless, because I get nothing from the transaction. This other, this nameless other, will be more important than I. But I feel better when I am not so self-centered. It directs my attention more to God and to his big world and not so much to myself. Then my problems and life are not so important and that frees me. If I am not so important, my mistakes are not so important. And when I am not the center I am not as alone.

In each case, the instructor's power to direct student behaviors outside class was used to invite specific forms of community attentiveness. Specific behaviors and time-patterned rituals were required of students (who were asked for their consent at the outset) and approached as a springboard to reflection and critical discussion, in keeping with the academic goals of the German course. This required some symbolic reframing and renegotiation of meaning in relation to pedagogy, since such activities were not what students usually associated with "homework"

---

19 Bonhoeffer, "Life Together 31".
20 David I. Smith, "Teaching Bonhoeffer: Pedagogy and Peripheral Practices," *International Journal of Christianity and Education* 21 (2017): 153. doi: 10.1177/2F2056997117700430.
21 Smith, "Teaching Bonhoeffer", 154.

or "assignments." Focusing on the invitation to formative practices contained in the assigned text led to a re-framing of what counted as classroom pedagogy in a German course.

As the above two examples illustrate, many student journal entries suggested a realization that even small-scale and short-term shifts in their intentional practices could have an effect. There was potential for such practices to significantly reframe their perception of others, opening fresh avenues for reflection and pathways toward maturation in their faith. Pedagogical design assisted in promoting these shifts. When the learning setting is approached not as a neutral backdrop within which faith is discussed, but rather as a complex environment within which formative practices can be shaped, academic learning and faith formation need not be at odds[22].

Narrative 3: On paper and in your hand
My third example shifts the focus from interpersonal behaviors to the materiality of the learning environment. It is drawn from an extensive empirical research project focused on patterns and consequences of digital technology use in Christian schools[23].

During a case study interview at a school heavily invested in teaching with digital media, a student expressed appreciation for one teacher's explicit insistence on using paper Bibles rather than digital access to Bible texts. The student offered the rationale that "for me, going forward in my life I want to be able to say, Oh I know where Judges is, and flip to it instead of being, like, I need to scroll through this until I find it or click it to get to it." This initial connection of paper Bibles to desired learning outcomes led to more extended reflections in the focus group on the connotations of the physical medium in which Scripture is encountered. In the ensuing conversation, one student mused[24]:

> I kind of like it because I like … how he forces us to use paper, because now it's just not on the computer and it's not one-dimensional. It's actually in your

---

22 Smith and Smith, Teaching and Christian Practices Julie E. Yonker, et al, 'Relational-based Christian Practices of Gratitude and Prayer Positively Impact Christian University Students' Reported Prosocial Tendencies,' *International Journal of Christianity & Education* 23 (2019): 150–170. doi: 10.1177/2056997119834044.
23 David I. Smith, et al, *Digital Life Together: The Challenge of Technology for Christian Schools* (Grand Rapids: Eerdmans, 2020).
24 Smith, *Digital Life Together*, 93.

hands and you are actually reading it on paper. Sometimes I think there's stuff that a computer can't really replicate. For me, reading it on paper, in your hand, is a lot more spiritual than actually just reading it on a screen. Well, I kind of feel like on a computer you have all these distractions and you get pop-ups and all that stuff and it kind of disrupts you and it's very easy to lose your focus whereas when you have a book, it's in your hands, you feel it, and you actually go and open it up and be, like, this is God's word and it's actually in your presence, not just on a computer screen.

A second student agreed[25]:

What I would probably say is that using a computer feels very high tech and new, and when you think about the Bible stories, you don't always think about them as super new. So when you get out a real book, a huge textbook kind of, you look at it—you feel like, you get the sense of this is God's word that someone wrote down specifically for me to read, like this is a big deal that it's sitting in front of me right now because these are God-breathed words. … It's no less important when you read it on a screen, but you don't get the same… there's been generations and generations of believers before me and this is an older way of doing things, but a way we should preserve.

Like other students in the study, these students expressed appreciation at being pressed into forms of engagement which they might not have chosen. In these student reflections, physical materials, aesthetics, and a specific sense of their positioning within time, within a narrative past, present, and future, are closely tied together and linked to the perceived power of the text to command reverence. The sheer physicality of the paper Bibles, as expressed in the act of opening them, their size and heft, their placement in the reader's hands, and the imposition of enduring marks on paper, evokes a specific configuration of time, aesthetics, and power[26].

Of course, other students may react differently. Neither these examples nor the research from which they are drawn offer a general case for the printed or against the digital. What they do illustrate is students sensing that the same words embedded in a different material resource may not generate quite the same learning experience.

---

25 Smith, *Digital Life Together*, 93.
26 Andrew Piper, *Book Was There: Reading in Electronic Times* (Chicago: University of Chicago Press, 2012).

Narrative 4: Going faster

A final example is drawn from the same research on technology use in Christian schools[27]. A recurring theme in focus group and case study interviews with teachers and students concerned how technology was affecting the flow of time. This concern appeared in various contexts. It was connected, for instance, with the pressures placed on teachers by student and parent expectations of swift email response, or the ways in which online availability of grades affected the rhythms of grading. The tendency of communication technologies to create pressures toward speed led some teachers to reflect on how what Heschel[28] refers to as the "architecture of time" might be impacting student formation. A religious educator in one school reflected[29] that

> Technology does a lot of things, really great things. One of the things that's maybe a negative is that it allows us to go faster, and to do more. I've kind of noticed with my students, I want to back off on that avenue a little bit. I don't always want to go faster, I don't always want to get through more of the Bible, sometimes I want to slow down and engage one part of the Bible really well, and to be slow, and to relieve some of the pressure of school.

We observed this teacher engaging in intentional classroom practices designed to communicate the value of slowing down, and of reading slowly and reflectively. These included creating opportunities for students to read alone in reflective silence, using pencil and paper to take notes, and verbally affirming students who did not get to the end of the assigned reading because of reflection on early sections of the reading. These classroom practices seemed consonant with an emphasis in wider discussions of "religious" or "spiritual" reading on the relationship between the ability to read slowly and attentively, the virtues of patience, humility, and justice, and faith formation[30].

---

27 Smith, *Digital Life Together*.
28 Abraham Joshua Heschel, *The Sabbath: Its Meaning for Modern Man* (New York: Farrar, Strauss & Company, 1951), 8.
29 Smith, *Digital Life Together*, 233.
30 David I. Smith, 'Reading Practices and Christian Pedagogy: Enacting Charity with Texts,' *Teaching and Christian Practices: Reshaping Faith and Learning*. Eds David I. Smith and James K. A. Smith. Grand Rapids: Eerdmans, 2011: 43-60; Paul Griffiths, *Religious Reading: The Place of Reading in the Practice of Religion* (New York: Oxford University Press, 1999).

At the same time, focus group research with students at the school revealed student awareness of patterns in school practices that pushed in the opposite direction. Students reported a tendency for technology to encourage skim reading, using search capabilities to go straight to an answer without reading the surrounding text, and copying answers from online sources without understanding them[31]. A pair of students reflected about homework in general[32]:

1 We'll ask [our teachers], "Can we just skim through for the answers" and they'll say, "No, I actually want you to read it." And … one of my teachers did that and I diligently read it and took notes … because I just do that. And I know a lot of people did because he actually emphasized that it's important to read it, whereas most teachers I get, I kind of skim it and look for the answers…
2 In other [classes] they just say, "Here's your reading assignment and then fill out the worksheet," and it is easy to just do Apple F and find where the answers are to each of the questions.

These students offer two different narratives about how homework works. At first, they suggest that "they" (i.e., teachers in general) emphasize careful reading, and the student then responds with careful reading simply because they are a good student, "because I just do that." Yet the first student only specifically recalls "one" of their teachers giving explicit attention in their instructions to how the homework was to be read. The second student suggests that the more typical behavior is an instruction that amounts to "here's your reading assignment and then fill out the worksheet." In those more common instances, both students report being less automatically virtuous in their reading behaviors. When the received message is that task completion is the purpose of the activity, digital technology offers efficient strategies to that end and encourages students to bypass of the slow, inefficient process of reading the whole text.

As we found more broadly in our study of technology use, teacher habits and material devices become mutually reinforcing. When students hear the message that productivity and completion are primary goals, and devices offer easy shortcuts, the pursuit of efficiency can displace deep engagement. Here again, a patterning of time, language and symbol use, and material resources has effects that touched on both academic

---

31 Smith, *Digital Life Together*, 234.
32 Smith, *Digital Life Together*, 235.

and spiritual formation. By touching upon both the capacity to understand deeply and the capacity to engage patiently and receptively with significant text, these patterns cut across distinctions between religious education and general education. They connect the learning environment per se to matters relevant to faith formation.

Conclusion
My intention here has not been to formulate generalized principles of faith formation; I intend a more modest outcome. I have focused on quite specific incidents within particular learning environments in order to show some of the ways in which faith formation does not "float in the air" in relation to pedagogical design. The bearing that education has on faith formation is not limited to the moments when prayers are being said or religion is to the topic of instruction. The design of general educational practices such as testing, grading, homework assignments, learning devices, and reading tasks are relevant. Faith formation unfolds within the complex environments in which teaching and learning are designed and experienced. The complexity and particularity of those environments suggests that the proper response may not be the construction of a fixed recipe for success. What is needed is the cultivation of an informed pedagogical attentiveness. Educators who care about faith formation should not think of it as something that happens only at special religious moments in the curriculum. Rather, they should approach the overall task of pedagogical design with attention to the formational nudges built into any design for learning.

Palmer[33] writes, "I must take responsibility for my mediator role, for the way my mode of teaching exerts a slow but steady formulative pressure on my students' sense of self and world," because "even secular education is a covert type of spiritual formation"[34]. The examples described here make this general point more concrete. Those concerned for the faith formation of learners need to cultivate attentiveness not only to how belief is explained and expressed, but to how educational practices are constructed and sustained. I have drawn a framework from Au's account of the various facets of curriculum as complex environmental design, suggesting that it might be helpful in drawing our attention to a more specific range of factors. Formation unfolds amid the interplay of material

---

33 Parker J. Palmer, "Education as Spiritual Formation," *Educational Horizons* 82 (2003): 65. http://www.jstor.org/stable/42926024
34 Palmer, "Spiritual Formation", 56.

and symbolic resources, the behaviors fostered, the aesthetic and temporal patterns that shape the experience of learning, and the ways in which the exercise of power constrains or enables the moves available. These processes are at work and helping to shape us whether or not faith is explicitly the topic of conversation. This picture need not imply a reduction of faith formation to material processes. In fact, it resists another modern reduction, namely the tendency to reduce pedagogy to the realm of efficient method and strategy, safely separate from the language of faith. Faith commitments are in play when we decide how to teach. Faith formation travels in contact with the earth.

3. What do we mean by Christian learning? Equipping Christian teachers for their vocation in public education.

Trevor Cooling

Introduction

The resignation of a British politician from the leadership of the Liberal Democratic Party following the General Election in June 2017 brought to the fore an underlying issue for Christians who seek to live under the authority of Scripture whilst actively participating in public life. Throughout the election campaign, Tim Farron, a theologically conservative evangelical Christian, was interrogated by journalists asking whether he thought gay sex was a sin. Knowing that whatever he said would be politically unhelpful, he never directly answered the question saying that his personal views on morality were irrelevant to his politics, adding that to "understand Christianity is to understand that we are all sinners"[1]. This did not deflect the journalists and eventually Farron resigned saying: "To be a political leader … and to live as a committed Christian, to hold faithfully to the Bible's teaching, has felt impossible."[2] In a subsequent lecture he expressed his frustration at what had happened saying: "And anyway, I was running for Prime Minister not Pope"![3]

Farron's resignation raises a number of questions about the tolerance of modern liberal society and how it deals with controversial issues,

---

1 Patrick Wintour, "Tim Farron Avoids Saying Whether He Sees Gay Sex As A Sin", *Guardian*, (18 July 2015). https://www.theguardian.com/politics/2015/jul/18/tim-farron-avoids-saying-whether-he-sees-gay-sex-as-a-sin
2 Quoted in Sophy Ridge, "Why Farron's faith is open to questions", *Metro*, June 16, 2017, 15.
3 *What Kind of Liberal Society Do We Want?* Lecture given at Theos on 28th November 2017. See https://www.theosthinktank.co.uk/events/2017/11/28/tim-farron-what-kind-of-liberal-society-do-we-want

questions that I have examined elsewhere[4]. In this chapter, I will focus on two other questions, namely:

1. What models of learning propagated in conservative Christian theology might have contributed to Farron's difficulties?
2. What features of conservative Christian theology might contribute to resolving Farron's difficulties?

Undoubtedly politics is a particularly challenging environment for Christians, but ethnographic research on evangelical churches in England suggests that the problem may be more generic . For example, Anna Strhan's in-depth study of two evangelical churches in London focused on how well congregational members felt each prepared them for engaging in public life as Christians.[5] One of the churches adopted what Strhan calls a traditional apologetics approach, where preparing members of the church to defend and contend for the objective truth of the Christian faith (and the anticipated opposition and conflict that will follow) was central to the discipleship programme[6]. The model of learning was a transmissionist one, aimed at ensuring that members knew the truths they were expected to advocate and defend. Strhan's interviews with its church members revealed "a sense of feeling awkward about speaking about faith in public contexts"[7] that was often associated with a sense of Farron-like shame at failure to achieve the hoped for stand-for-truth.

Strhan's findings are echoed in research conducted at my own university, which investigated how secondary school teachers from a range of subject disciplines working in church schools responded to the challenge to teach in a distinctively Christian way.[8] Some of the teachers

---

4 Trevor Cooling, "What Is A Controversial Issue? Implications for the Treatment of Religious Beliefs in Education," *Journal of Beliefs and Values* 33:2 (2012), 169-181.
5 Anna Strhan, *Aliens and Strangers: The Struggle for Coherence in the Everyday Lives of Evangelicals* (Oxford: Oxford University Press, 2015a) and "Negotiating the Public and the Private in Everyday Evangelicalism" in Titus Hjelm (ed) *Is God Back?: Reconsidering the New Visibility of Religion* (London: Bloomsbury, 2015b), 77-89.
6 Christian Smith describes this as a Biblicist approach. See *The Bible Made Impossible: Why Biblicism Is Not a Truly Evangelical Reading of Scripture* (Grand Rapids: Brazos Press, 2012) 3-6 for a discussion of its characteristics.
7 Strhan, "Negotiating" 83
8 Trevor Cooling with Beth Green, Andrew Morris and Lynn Revell, *Christian Faith in English Church Schools: Research Conversations with Classroom Teachers* (Bern: Peter Lang, 2016)

found the challenge 'weird', because they could not see how the approach that they perceived was required in their classrooms in order to be biblically-faithful resonated with what they perceived to be their professional responsibilities as teachers. In a nutshell, they assumed that Christians had to act as apologists in the public arena of education, their main purpose being to witness so as to persuade their students to accept established Christian truths. They seemed to assume that Christian learning entails being told and then accepting Christian truths, whereas their instincts as teachers was that learning happened best in enquiry-based approaches. One maths teacher commented that she felt she was required to shoe-horn God into her lessons by just "banging in a plenary"[9]. It was this approach that she described as "weird". Her reactions were mirrored by other teachers in the research. The evidence from this piece of research is that the teachers participating did not always find the Christian faith helpful in developing their understanding of their professional role as promoters of learning[10].

This leads me to the central question of this chapter: 'What do we mean by Christian learning?' In particular I will explore the (unhelpful) perception that is emerging from this research that there is a conflict between learning that is biblically-faithful and the model of learning that is professionally normative in secular education. My aim is to identify a model of Christian learning that would better equip the likes of Tim Farron for effective engagement as professionals in a world that may be unsympathetic to Christian faith.

Learning and Authority

The research of Ruth Deakin Crick and Helen Jelfs into the relationship between spirituality and learning throws some initial light on our question.[11] In their view the key issue is where authority is seen to lie in

---

9   Cooling, *Church Schools*, 88.
10 See also Hazel Bryan & Lynn Revell, "Performativity, Faith and Professional Identity: Student Religious Education Teachers and the Ambiguities of Objectivity", *British Journal of Educational Studies*, 59(4), (2011) 403-419.
11 Ruth Deakin Crick and Helen Jelfs *Spirituality, Learning and Personalisation: Exploring the Relationship between Spiritual Development and Learning How to Learn. Report for Advisory Board on phase 2.* (Bristol: Graduate School of Education, Bristol University, 2011a) and Ruth Deakin Crick and Helen Jelfs "Spirituality, Learning and Personalisation: Exploring the Relationship between Spiritual Development and Learning to Learn in a Faith-based Secondary School", *International Journal of Children's Spirituality* 16(3) (2011b) 197-217

the learning process, distinguishing between what they called self-authorship and external authority for learning. In the latter, learning is controlled by an outsider like a teacher, whereas in the former learners create meaningful knowledge for themselves. This latter idea is what I shall call the *pedagogical priority* and reflects the widespread professional concern that learning ought to be enquiry-based and constructed by the learner. For Deakin Crick and Jelfs, self-authorship represents spiritually-infused learning and resonates with the constructivist approaches to teaching which are influential in modern educational thought. Their conclusion seems to challenge the belief that learning can be directed by an external, higher authority. For theologically conservative Christian teachers it therefore seems difficult to see how they can both hold belief in an authoritative Bible that should control learning and accept the pedagogical priority of self-authorship in learning. Hence they find the idea of distinctively Christian learning appears 'weird'. Like Tim Farron in his professional political context, such teachers simply do not know how to speak the faith in this professional educational context. Yet the belief that the Bible is authoritative is central to orthodox Christian teaching. In this paper I shall explore this sense of dissonance and suggest a resolution by exploring what is meant by Christian learning[12].

Criticisms of a Conservative View of the Bible

The problems perceived by critics of those holding a conservative view of the Bible were summarised by the philosopher Peter Vardy when he wrote: "The problem with the Bible ......as an authority is that so much depends on how the text is read and the interests of the reader" [13]. In his analysis of the difference between good and bad religion, Vardy argues that text-based religions are particularly dangerous because they engender what John Hull called "religionism", an attitude that nurtures rejection, exclusion and tribalism when encountering views different from its own.[14]

---

12 Other traditions may offer different case studies of the role of authority. For example within the Roman Catholic tradition the authority of the Church would be more central and in Islam the authority of the Qur'an. The reflections offered in this chapter specifically apply to conservative Protestant approaches to the Bible but hopefully might stimulate thinking about authority and learning in other traditions.
13 Peter Vardy, *Good & Bad Religion* (London: SCM, 2010) 79
14 Vardy, *Religion*, 98 & 173. See also John Hull, "Editorial", *British Journal of Religious Education*, 14(2) (1992), 69-72 and in *Utopian Whispers: Moral, Religious and Spiritual Values in Schools* (Norwich: Religious and Moral Education Press, 1998), 54-58.

But this is not the only problem. Elsewhere John Hull observed that "in a changing world, an unchanging theology soon becomes irrelevant", which means that those that consider that they have access to God's authoritative, presumably unchanging, Word are, in the face of new situations and new knowledge, either left with a beached theology or have to mount a defensive action to preserve its integrity[15]. He argues that this leads either to a puerile faith or to abandonment of faith. It makes it impossible, as Tim Farron concluded, to live with integrity in the wider, secular world. For teachers, the question then becomes how their duty to fulfil their professional responsibility to promote learning is to be fulfilled when their over-riding loyalty is to transmitting God's authoritative word? Hull's point is that change and learning are intimately related and teachers who hold to what they perceive as unchanging, authoritative, biblical teaching find themselves in an uncomfortable position if required to promote an approach to learning where students develop new insights rather than simply being the passive recipients of fixed and time-less truths.

Christopher Rowlands and Jonathan Roberts develop this criticism of conservative approaches to the Bible claiming that they create a "baton exchange mentality" in regard to teaching and learning. [16] This entails a pedagogical approach where the expert exegete discerns the fixed meanings of the text, the theologian systematizes them and then the preacher and teacher apply them to life situations in modern contexts, with the learner absorbing the resulting orthodox teaching as the final step in a linear, transmission model of learning. Here the Bible is treated as the "univocal, authoritative text", the "final word" or "court of appeal"[17] and learning is perceived as top-down transmission resulting in the successful reception of authorized, authoritative meanings. In contrast Rowlands and Roberts wish to emphasise the importance of the context within which the text is read as a key influence in shaping what is learnt from the text and of the role of the Spirit in creating new and radical meanings which may transcend the text itself. Furthermore, in the spirit of self-authorship, they assert the desirability of 'sinners' interpreting the

---

15 John Hull, *Studies in Religion and Education* (Brighton: Falmer Press, 1984), 208. See also his extended discussion in *What Prevents Christian Adults from Learning?* (London: SCM, 1985)

16 Christopher Rowlands and Jonathan Roberts, *The Bible for Sinners* (London: SPCK, 2008), 36

17 Rowlands and Roberts, *Sinners*, 13 & 15

text for themselves and deny the need for a hierarchy of approved experts to ensure the correct meaning is discerned. Indeed they regard such experts as exercising their power in an act of oppression through their control of authoritative textual meanings[18]. They no doubt would agree with John Hull when he criticized conservative models of biblical interpretation that claim ownership of authorized meanings saying:

> It is as if squatters have taken up residence in this vast mansion, which is really public property, and refuse to let anyone in, unless they become like the people who have already squatted there. [19]

For Rowlands and Roberts, the text is a catalyst for interpretation and a gateway to personal understanding for learners, not a source of given meanings to be delivered by authorized teachers irrespective of the receiving context. [20] They therefore criticize those who "consistently return conservative answers from a set of Gospels that are essentially a profoundly radical set of texts"[21] and, instead, champion radical uses of the Bible. Here is how they describe their position.

> The model we advocate.....looks past this hierarchical hermeneutic, and seeks to find ongoing, contingent understandings of Christianity within the messiness and compromised 'sinfulness' of everyday life[22]

John Hull's solution is for Christians to treat the Bible as an illuminating rather than an adjudicating text. [23]

Hull, Rowlands and Roberts are here expressing concerns about a baton-passing pedagogy that treats the Bible as authoritatively God's word. In their view, Christians who adopt this will struggle to embrace the pedagogical priority that learning in the religious domain should accommodate self-authorship and the resulting diversity of interpretation.

---

18 Rowlands and Roberts, *Sinners*, 23
19 John M Hull, "The Bible in the Secular Classroom: An Approach Through the Experience of Loss", I Astley, J & day, D (eds.), *The Contours of Christian Education* (Great Wakering: McCrimmons, 1992). 201.
20 Rowlands and Roberts, *Sinners*, 85
21 Rowlands and Roberts, *Sinners*, 31
22 Rowlands and Roberts, *Sinners*, 25
23 John M Hull, "Christian Theology and Educational Theory: Can There be Connections?", British Journal of Educational Studies, xxiv, (1976) 127-143. Reprinted in John M Hull Studies in Religion and Education (Lewes:Falmer Press, 1984), 229-247

The research data described at the start of this chapter certainly suggests that they have identified an important challenge for Bible-believing Christian educators. But is it really the case that there is no theologically conservative approach to biblical interpretation that both respects biblical authority and embraces self-authorship in Christian learning?

A Constructivist Approach

The pedagogical priority of self-authorship identified by Deakin Crick and Jelfs resonates with what is often referred to as a constructivist approach to learning by other authors. Clive Erricker and Michael Grimmitt, influential British advocates of constructivism in religious education, describe it as follows:

> At root it identifies knowledge as a human construct which is the consequence of the way in which individuals and communities order their experience. As such what is conceived as "knowledge" does not and cannot reflect some "objective", ontological reality because that is unknowable. Human knowledge, as a consequence, reflects the way in which individuals order and organise their experience of the world, using concepts which fit the situations they encounter. A characteristic of human knowledge...is that it is subject to multiple interpretations or 'constructs' and is controversial or problematic by nature.[24]

This quotation clearly embraces the concept of self-authorship highlighting "the necessary involvement of the learner, as a situated and contextualized individual in the construction of learning"[25]. Their constructivism challenges the instructional models of learning valued by those religious communities who wish education to transmit the content authorized by their community. In contrast to this, Erricker argues for the superiority of what he calls relativism. He is worried by those religions that claim to own the *true* grand narrative because, in so doing, their *faith* becomes an exclusivist and oppressive *ideology* [26]. In contrast, for him

---

24 Clive Erricker, *Religious Education: a Conceptual and Interdisciplinary Approach for Secondary Level*, (Abingdon, David Fulton Books, 2010) 78 and Clive Erricker, Judith Lowndes and Elaine Bellchambers, *Primary Religious Education – A New Approach*, (Abingdon: Routledge, 2011) 59-60 both quoting from Michael Grimmitt, *Pedagogies of Religious Education* (Great Wakering: McCrimmons, 2000) 208

25 Grimmitt, *Pedagogies*, 225.

26 Clive and Jane Erricker, *Reconstructing Religious, Spiritual and Moral Education*, London: Routledge, 2000), 10 (Emphases mine.) This distinction between faith and

learning is regarded as "constructing and voicing our own fictions within a listening community".[27] Therefore Erricker presents the teacher with a stark choice: "He or she. ....must side with the relativists or accept the 'native' view"....and thereby place themselves on "one side of the fence or the other".[28] Siding with the relativists means accepting that "no narrative does more than serve its own ends for the community for which it proves useful"(p. 34)[29]. This clearly has huge implications for Christian teachers who are 'natives' in their approach to the authority of the Bible and are, therefore, apparently on the wrong side of the fence. If adopted as professionally normative in education, Erricker's radical constructivism (as I choose to call it) would make it impossible for Bible-following Christian teachers to work with integrity. It allows no place for biblical authority in learning. Grimmitt is more circumspect and merely comments that it would be unfortunate if teachers' personal theological assumptions became "the major determinant" of how they reacted to the challenge of constructivism.[30] However neither Grimmitt nor Erricker offers advice to Christians who accept biblical authority as to how they do this, other than to convert to relativism and abandon their conservative convictions. This clearly has significant outcomes for Christian teachers in implying that one must be relativist in order to be a fully professional. In his later work Erricker acknowledges this problem and, following Grimmitt's lead, distinguishes between his preferred radical technical constructivism and what he calls a broad constructivist approach.[31] This, he claims, gives careful attention to the quality of the interaction of the student with the religious content being studied by embracing open enquiry rather than instruction, but does not require acceptance of relativism. However he never offers a non-relativist understanding of

---

ideology is central to Erricker's thesis. His position is unashamedly non-realist and rests on the distinction between "a believer's faith and knowledge as an epistemological claim or ideology" (*Reconstructing*, 2000, p. 61). For detailed discussion of this point see pages 65 and 74. See also my review article on this book: Trevor Cooling, "Reconstructing Religious, Spiritual and Moral Education", *Journal of Beliefs and Values*, 23(1), (2002) 107-111.

27 Errickers, *Reconstructing*, 9
28 Errickers, *Reconstructing*, 33
29 Clive Erricker, "Shall We Dance? Authority, Representation and Voice: The Place of Spirituality in Religious Education", *Religious Education*, 96 (1), (2001), 34.
30 Grimmitt, *Pedagogies*, 225
31 Erricker, *Religious*, 78-79.

religion that resonates with these broad-constructivist, pedagogical aspirations. This still leaves Farron with his problem.

The question is whether Bible-believing Christian teachers can appropriate any insights from the broad constructivist suggestion as they grapple with understanding Christian learning. Must Christian teachers abandon traditional approaches to biblical authority and embrace the radical constructivist approach that makes the learner's response the authority if they are to move beyond transmissionist teaching and be able to embrace the pedagogical priority given to self-authorship in learning? Will they be able to accept in constructing meaning, the necessity of change in religious learning, the influence of the learner's context and the inevitability of treating a diversity of views emerging as legitimately controversial without denying biblical authority? It is these questions that the secondary teachers described earlier were tacitly struggling with.

We can begin to understand what an alternative, biblically-friendly constructivist understanding to what is meant by this 'constructing and voicing' in response to text might look like from an interview with Dominic Dromgoole, the Artistic Director at Shakespeare's Globe Theatre in London. [32] Discussing his childhood, he said that growing up without religion meant that he needed another "big canonical thing". The works of Shakespeare played this role for him which he described as "emitting generous, warm, brilliant energy". He used them to help him understand himself and the wider world. They acted as a guide to his life. He contrasted this experience to what often happened in schools where it was assumed that certain "priests" (i.e. his teachers) understood Shakespeare while the rest, who did not, sat in dumb silence as the priests told them what it meant. Dromgoole was here advocating a version of a constructivist approach to Shakespeare and condemning a view of the text which sought to transmit authorized and authoritative meanings, but which took seriously the idea of 'canonical' status for the text. What might that mean?

Drawing on this thought, the rest of this chapter will explore an alternative approach to constructivism and the Bible that embraces the pedagogical priority but without conceding the relativism inherent in radical constructivism. This will draw on Erricker's notion of a broad constructivist approach whilst affirming the authority of the biblical

---

32 From *Lenny Henry on Shakespeare*, broadcast on 1st April 2012 on ITV1

(canonical) text as God's revelatory word[33]. It will suggest that the shift necessary for Christian teachers is to move from seeing learning as an exercise in transmission and persuasion that draws on the theological discipline of apologetics, to seeing learning as an exercise in promoting insightful interpretation that draws on the theological discipline of hermeneutics[34]. In undertaking this task, I will interact with conservative theologians who seek to honour the authority of the Bible in line with Tim Farron's aspiration.

Responsible Hermeneutics and Learning [35]
In the rest of this chapter, I will argue that the way to support teachers who accept the authority of the Bible in their pursuit of the pedagogical priority is not to deconstruct their faith and identity as evangelical Christians as Hull, Grimmitt and, particularly, Erricker apparently want to do, but rather to explore with them a credible understanding of what it means to be *faithful* to the Bible in developing an appropriate theology of learning[36]. The British theologian Alister McGrath invokes the concept of the organic theologian to describe someone adopting this approach. He describes such a person as seeing:

> …himself (sic) working within the great historical Christian tradition which he makes his own. Even when he feels he must critique the contemporary expressions or applications of that tradition, he will do so from a deep sense of commitment to the community of faith and its distinctive ideas and values.[37]

---

[33] I agree with Tom Wright in seeing the phrase "the authority of Scripture" as shorthand for "the authority of the triune God, exercised somehow through Scripture". This is a significant nuance with consequences for how the Bible is viewed. See N.T. Wright, *Scripture and the Authority of God* (London: SPCK, 2005). 17 & 92.

[34] Note that I will not be arguing that apologetics is an illegitimate enterprise per se. Rather I will argue that it is not the most helpful theological discipline to draw upon for thinking about Christian learning, particularly in schools.

[35] See also my "Curiosity: vice or virtue for the Christian teacher" *Journal of Education of Christian Belief*, 9(2) (2005), 87-103.

[36] See Clive Erricker, "Shall We Dance? Authority, Representation and Voice: The Place of Spirituality in Religious Education", *Religious Education*, 96 (1), (2001), 20-35.In contrast see Steven Garber, *The Fabric of Faithfulness (expanded edition)*, (Downers Grove: IVP, 2007) and James D Hunter, *To Change the World*, (Oxford, OUP, 2010). Both employ the concept of faithfulness as the marker of a Christian approach to life.

[37] Alister McGrath, *The Future of Christianity*, (Oxford: Blackwell, 2002) 152. Kevin Vanhoozer also uses this idea derived from Antonio Gramsci to illuminate his concept

My argument will be that Christian teachers who accept the authority of the Bible and who are organic theologians will desire to be faithful to the Bible and that faithfulness, understood properly, will embrace the pedagogical priority and manifest "creative fidelity".[38] The problem is, as we have seen from qualitative research, that many such Christians interpret faithfulness as obligating them to adopt Rowland's and Roberts' 'baton exchange' mentality to learning with the aim of persuading students to accept a biblical view, rather than adopt one which respects their students and themselves as self-authoring interpreters. The missiological theologian Christopher J.H. Wright dubs this as a "military-style command" understanding of the authority of Scripture that thereby treats the Bible as a proverbial sergeant-major who barks orders that the hapless squaddies must follow to the letter whatever[39]. This makes aspirations like the creativity of self-authorship, recognition of the impact of the reader's context, critical thought leading to a change in view and acceptance of diversity of interpretations in response to reading the Bible appear problematic. Deep in their psyche, it appears that conservative Christian teachers think that they must favour a transmissionist or apologetic approach to learning[40]. However Strhan's research and Farron's experience suggests that this sets up failure and creates a culture of guilt and shame. Furthermore, it is also common for critics to assume that faithfulness to biblical authority entails a literalist approach and allows them to dismiss it without any serious consideration[41]. With increasing

of the everyday theologian. See *Everyday Theology*, (Grand Rapids: Baker Academic, 2007) 57. Richard Briggs develops this notion of faithfulness in a different way by examining the virtues that are desirable in a "virtuous" reader of the Old Testament. See *The Virtuous Reader: Old Testament Narrative and Interpretive Virtue*, (Grand Rapids,: Baker Academic, 2010).

38 Kevin Vanhoozer, *Is There a Meaning in This Text?* (Leicester, IVP,1998) 388
39 Christopher Wright, *The Mission of God: Unlocking the Bible's Grand Narrative* (Downers Grove: IVP, 2006), 52
40 I explored the distinction between apologetic and hermeneutical approaches in my 2010 paper presented to the Anglican Education Commission in Sydney. In that I drew on the case study undertaken by Elizabeth Green in *An Ethnographic Study of a CTC with a Bible-based Ethos* (Unpublished D.Phil. Thesis. Oxford: University of Oxford, 2009). See Trevor Cooling, *Distinctively Christian School Leadership: wishful thinking or practical reality? An English Case Study*, Sydney: Anglican Education Commission, 6th September 2010.
41 E.g. Richard Dawkins, *The God Delusion,* (London: Black Swan, 2006); Michael Hand, "Should we teach homosexuality as a controversial issue?", *Theory and Research in Education*, 5, (2007), 69-86; Richard Norman, *On Humanism, (*Abingdon: Routledge, 2004).

concerns about religious extremism, it also means that the biblically faithful can easily be stereotyped as a fundamentalist threat.

There is a significant distinction that needs introducing at this point. Conservative Christians are realists not relativists, by which is meant that they believe that the Bible teaches universal truth to which all are accountable. But there is an important distinction between *naïve* realist approaches and those that are *critical* realist. The key distinction is that the latter embrace insights from post-modernism in regard to the subjectivity and situatedness of the learner whereas the former do not. Amongst British Christian scholars who write on religious education, probably the most well-known exponent of critical realism is Andrew Wright[42]. He outlines three defining features of critical realism[43], which I have listed below and to which I have added some implications for an approach to reading the Bible:

1. Ontological realism - meaning that there is an external truth to be known which is communicated through the text by the human author and which is legitimately viewed as 'God's word' and is therefore authoritative. This means that the idea that the text has an intended meaning makes sense. It cannot just mean anything that the reader wants to make it mean.
2. Epistemic relativism – meaning that access to that truth is always mediated through situated, human interpretive activity and therefore entails subjectivity. This is the valid insight that has come from post-modernism. It leads to an awareness of the fallibility of the interpreter and a degree of epistemic humility in holding the interpretations we are personally convinced by.
3. Judgemental rationality – meaning that discerning the truth conveyed by the text is dependent on critical enquiry into and judgement of the validity of the interpretations made by different people.

---

42 E.g. Andrew Wright, *Critical Religious Education, Multiculturalism and the Pursuit of Truth*, (Cardiff, University of Cardiff Press, 2007) and *Christianity and Critical Realism* (Abingdon: Routledge, 2013). N.T. Wright is an influential theologian who has embraced a critical realist approach. See, for example, his *New Testament and the People of God*, (London, SPCK, 1992). For an example of a Christian educationalist who embraces critical realism see Richard Edlin, "In pursuit of an authentic Christian paradigm; the place of reformed critical realism" in Richard Edlin and Jill Ireland (eds) *Engaging the Culture: Christians at Work in Education* (Sydney: National Institute for Christian Education, 2006) 91-108.

43 Wright, *Christianity*, 10-16. These are sometimes called the holy trinity of critical realism.

A naïve realist will focus on ontological realism and ignore the other two dimensions. In relation to the Bible they therefore assume that discerning the meaning of the text is an objective task, akin to science. The naïve realist believes that God speaks directly and unmediated through the perspicuous text to the believer who receives its meaning. The task of the Christian learner is then to receive this from their teacher. [44] The presumably apocryphal story of the college principal admonishing one of his argumentative students in a theology class by saying 'young man, you are arguing with God', illustrates this attitude to learning the Bible. A critical realist will, however, assume that there is considerable work to be done in interpreting the text if it is to be understood correctly. Unlike the naïve realist, she will also be considerably more cautious about asserting that her interpretation *is* God's word, recognizing that her inescapable subjectivity and contextual situatedness makes her interpretations of the text contestable. She will also recognise that although Bible passages may have a clear meaning, the significance of that meaning in different contemporary contexts may well be legitimately varied.[45] In other words she will regard consideration of her own context as being as important of consideration as the context of the original biblical author[46]. The critical realist Bible reader will therefore treat faithful Christian learning as a relatively complex task involving a balance between careful exegesis of the meaning of the text and creative discernment of the significance of the text in contemporary contexts.[47] This is in stark contrast to the naïve realist reader of biblical texts who will assume that faithful Christian learning entails receiving established meanings with obvious significance.

Alister McGrath sees the clash between the naïve realist and critical realist approaches as underlying the fundamental divide that exists in conservative scholarship, contrasting, by example, the work of Wayne Grudem and Kevin Vanhoozer[48]. The latter is an exponent of the art of

---

44 In Cooling, *Church Schools*, I argue that this is attributable to the influence of positivism on evangelical thought.
45 Kevin Vanhoozer, *Meaning*, 421-424,
46 Commonly referred to as the two horizons; the horizon of the text and the horizon of the reader.
47 See Mark Allan Powell, *Chasing the Eastern Star: Adventures in Biblical Reader Response Criticism*, (Westminster John Knox Press, 2001) for a fascinating discussion of the different significances to be discerned in Matthew's parable of the Prodigal Son
48 Alister McGrath, "Evangelical Theological Method: The State of the Art" in John G. Stackhouse Jr (ed.), *Evangelical Futures: A Conversation on Theological Method* (Grand Rapids: Baker Books, 2000)

hermeneutics which grapples with exactly what is happening when Christians follow biblical texts, whereas the former treats Bible passages as "timeless and culture-free statements that can be assembled to create a timeless and culture-free theology that stands over and above the shifting sands of our postmodern culture"[49]. Richard Bauckham echoes Vanhoozer approach when he writes:

> In order to relate the Bible to the contemporary world, we need both interpretation of Scripture and an interpretation of the contemporary world. We cannot just repeat what our predecessors said to very different contexts in the past… Too many Christian attempts to open up the Bible's relevance today or to draw on the resources of the Bible in order to address the contemporary world lack this crucial element of contextuality.[50]

At the same time, but unlike the radical constructivist, the critical realist will see meaning as flowing from the text to her and not just from her into the text. She will therefore treat the text as of intrinsic worth with an intended meaning and not just as an instrumental catalyst in the construction of her own narrative. She will, however, also recognize that the new questions generated by the new contexts which readers inhabit may well generate new significances for the text. For the purposes of this discussion, the important feature of a critical realist approach to the Bible is the belief that God speaks *authoritatively* revealing meaning through the text and contextually as the learner discerns the significance of that meaning thereby giving credence to the belief that it is possible to hear His voice if appropriate care is taken. The text, therefore, "remains in control" interrogating and constraining the reader in their role of enquirer.[51] It is adjudicating and not just illuminating. As a learner, the reader sits under the text benefitting from its insights as she seeks to discern its significance in different contexts, rather than over and against the text adjudicating on its value. In the model that I am proposing, *self-authorship in learning is therefore constrained by the external authority of the text.*[52]

---

49 McGrath, "Method", 30.
50 Richard Bauckham *The Bible in the Contemporary World: Hermeneutical Ventures* (Grand Rapids: Eerdmans, 2015) ix.
51 Anthony Thiselton, *Hermeneutics: An Introduction*, (London: SPCK, 2009), 8
52 Richard Briggs describes this as a hermeneutics of trust in *The Virtuous Reader: Old Testament Narrative and Interpretive Virtue*, (Grand Rapids: Baker Academic, 2010).

A helpful metaphor for what is happening when Christians seek to learn from Scripture is offered by the missiologist Christopher Wright.[53] He considers the activity of cartographers who draw maps to represent the reality of the terrain. He argues that inevitably these are distortions in not representing that terrain exactly as it is in every detail. He cites the example of the world famous map of the London Underground system. When training Christian teachers it always intrigues me that on being asked whether this map is true, many say no. This appears to be because it is not a literal representation. Yet they continue to rely on it to get around London because, as Wright says, "In its own terms, the London Underground map is a comprehensively accurate document".[54] In other words, although this map is not a literal representation of London terrain, it is a true representation in that its focus is on serving a particular purpose whilst staying faithful to the terrain. Paddington cannot represented as east of Kings Cross! Similarly, in learning from the Bible Christians are creating interpretations of the text that are often responses to issues and questions arising from their own context. To use Wright's metaphor, they are drawing a map for a particular purpose. For it to be a true interpretation of the text it does not have to be literal repeat of the text and it must be creative in offering a contextually helpful response, but it cannot distort the meaning of the text in ways that clearly are contrary to Scripture itself. Learning to do this well is what constitutes Christian learning.

This understanding of being faithful as a Christian learner resonates with Anthony Thiselton's concept of *responsible hermeneutics* and offers a way forward for conceptualising learning that enables Christian teachers to draw on the helpful insights associated with the pedagogical priority whilst remaining faithful to their own commitment to biblical authority.[55] In other words Thiselton offers a way for Christians to reframe the notion of pedagogical priority rather than to reject it outright or embrace it uncritically. Thiselton maintains that the distinction between exegesis and hermeneutics is that in hermeneutics one asks "exactly what are we

---

53 Wright, *Mission*, 68-69.
54 Wright, *Mission*, 69.
55 Thiselton, *Hermeneutics*. For an application of his notion of responsible hermeneutics to the development of a resource for teaching Christianity in schools see Stephen Pett and Trevor Cooling "Understanding Christianity: Exploring a Hermeneutical Pedagogy for Teaching Christianity", *British Journal of Religious Education,* 40(3), (2018)

doing when we read, understand and apply texts?"⁵⁶ His answer challenges the oft-made assumption that exegesis is a science that enables one to unearth the objective, timeless meaning of a text. Rejecting this positivism, he argues that every reader approaches the text with a "pre-understanding", which he describes as "an initial and provisional stage in the journey towards understanding something more fully".⁵⁷ So no-one reads a text totally 'objectively' in the naïve realist sense. There is always a subjective process of constructing meaning which draws on one's worldview, reflects one's cultural situatedness and often serves one's own interests. His view is that the existence of such pre-understandings is simply a fact of life, namely that we all interpret from somewhere; he argues that this is not inherently threatening to the enterprise of discovering truth, but it does have to be taken into account in seeking to learn as a biblically faithful learner.

Thiselton's notion of responsible hermeneutics leads, I suggest, to seeing the importance of holding two activities in balance, which together enable the learner to participate in the oft-discussed hermeneutical circle.⁵⁸ These are the hermeneutics of retrieval whereby the interpreter seeks to discern the intended meaning of the text through critical study of its background, language, symbols, metaphors, meanings and narratives and a hermeneutics of suspicion where the pre-understanding and interests of the reader and his/her shaping community/ies are examined.⁵⁹ Central to responsible hermeneutics is that the conclusions reached by interpreters on the basis of their pre-understandings are ultimately constrained by the results of the retrieval process and are inevitably open to challenge. The text cannot be made to mean simply anything⁶⁰. In the process of Christian learning, critical judgements have therefore to be made about the validity, creativity and wisdom of our interpretations. This best happens in a community context where

---

56 Thiselton, *Hermeneutics*, 4
57 Thiselton, *Hermeneutics*, 12
58 This is better understood as a spiral according to Thiselton because this metaphor acknowledges that there is growth in understanding as text and reader interact with each other (*Hermeneutics*, 15). Erricker uses the hermeneutical circle in his recent work on a conceptual approach to RE, but it is unclear whether he would accept the spiral metaphor which would imply the possibility of growth in knowledge. See Erricker 2010 and 2011.
59 Thiselton, *Hermeneutics*, 19.
60 Anthony Thiselton, *Can the Bible Mean Whatever We Want It to Mean?* (Chester: Chester Academic Press, 2005).

judgemental rationality is practised in the context of a shared commitment to biblical faithfulness.

A Practical Example
The approach to learning that arises from responsible hermeneutics is skilfully captured in the New Testament theologian NT Wright's widely-cited analogy where he compares living under the authority of the biblical text with the task of completing a newly discovered but unfinished Shakespeare play[61]. Wright asks us to imagine how experienced Shakespearean actors would go about this task. He suggests two significant insights. First, they would seek to be faithful to the thrust of the narrative of the unfinished play and to Shakespeare's wider corpus of writing, which acts as an authority. Their suggested completion of the play must be justifiably Shakespearian, a concept which acts as an authoritative constraint on the actors' creativity[62]. Second, they would need to be creative in writing the new text and this creativity would inevitably reflect their own situated, contextual setting and personal interests. Wright argues that Christians seeking to live their lives under the authority of Scripture face a similar task to these Shakespearean actors. The analogy affirms acceptance of the Bible as authoritatively God's word, but replaces the literalist, militaristic conception of unthinking obedience to commands with faithfulness to the Bible as a shaping narrative[63]. It requires Christians to show creativity if they really are to live under the

---

61 See N.T. Wright, *The New Testament and the People of God*, (London: SPCK, 1992), 139-143. For citations of this analogy see, Brian Walsh & J Richard Middleton, *Truth is Stranger than it Used to Be,* (London: SPCK, 1995), Craig Bartholomew & Michael Goheen, *The Drama of Scripture: Finding our Place in the Biblical Story*, (Grand Rapids: Baker Academic, 2004) and Rowlands & Roberts, *Sinners*. Note my description here is truncated and thereby misses many of the nuances of Wright's original and the subsequent discussion of it.

62 The authority of the text does not then primarily reside in individual propositions, but in the overall narrative or storyline. Many would say that the text of the Bible as a whole should be interpreted through the lens of the Christian gospel. The Bible is therefore viewed as a coherent sacred text with a unified message which acts as the means of God's revelation. However within this unified message there are many discernible themes or theologies, which can illuminate the readers understanding, but over-reliance on one can distort the text by ignoring the others.

63 See also Christopher Wright "The ethical authority of biblical social vision" in Michael Schulter & John Ashcroft (eds.) *Jubilee Manifesto; a Framework, Agenda and Strategy for Christian Social Reform* (Nottingham: IVP, 2005) 67-81.

authority of their shaping text. Wright calls it 'improvising'.[64] In other words it entails a constructivist, learning relationship with the text in order to be faithful to its authority. This, I suggest, is what Dominic Dromgoole meant by referring to Shakespeare's plays as his canon – a set of authoritative narratives that guided him in life, although clearly in his case this did not amount to Divine revelation as it does with the Bible.

What difference, then, might this proposed theological approach make to a Christian understanding of learning? I will conclude with one example drawn from a research project where 14 secondary school teachers employed in English church schools were studied intensively for one year to see how they responded to the challenge to promote distinctively Christian learning.[65] Angela was a teacher of Religious Education who was highly successful in the results she achieved in public examinations. The research team worked with her on a unit in a Christian ethics course for 15 year-olds focused on the debate about assisted suicide. She showed great skill in preparing the students for examination questions that required them to rehearse three reasons in favour of and three reasons against assisted suicide. Typically the three reasons for were taken from Christians and were backed with Bible verses; the three reasons against often came from secularist literature. In a discussion of this approach Angela was asked what her students might imagine Christian ethics was all about having been taught in this way. It came home to her that the students were probably learning that Christian ethics is primarily concerned with winning arguments on single issues by deploying isolated Bible verses against one's secular opponents. This was a very upsetting realisation for her.

She then turned to the work of Luke Bretherton whose doctoral thesis had focused on the New Testament Gospels response to ethical debates.[66] His conclusion was that, working from the Gospel narratives, the overriding sense is that the first Christian response to ethical dispute is not immediately plan strategies to win the argument but rather to prioritise expressing love and compassion towards those with whom one is in dispute. Angela therefore sought to reframe the learning experience

---

64 N.T. Wright, *Scripture and the Authority of God: How to Read the Bible Today* (London: SPCK, 2005), 91-93. Kevin Vanhoozer describes this as creating "forms of life that correspond to the biblical text in contemporary contexts" in *Everyday Theology*), 55.
65 Cooling, et al, *Church Schools*, 77-80
66 Luke Bretherton, *Hospitality as Holiness: Christian Witness Amid Moral Diversity*, (Aldershot: Ashgate, 2006)

of her students using this insight. She turned to the story of Tony Nicklinson, well-known in the British media.[67] Nicklinson had suffered a massive stroke at the age of fifty that turned him from an active man to a sufferer of locked-in syndrome. He was a prominent campaigner for the right to assisted suicide. Angela redesigned her students' learning experience by focusing on his story emphasising the importance of the loving action of listening carefully to him before making a judgment. She then took her students through a learning process where they investigated the concerns of those who opposed Nicklinson's campaign, for example disability campaigners who were anxious about the impact of available euthanasia on their community. Then the students reviewed the debate before working on the three arguments for and three arguments against assisted suicide required by the exam. She had therefore moved to an approach that focussed on narratives rather than isolated points.

This example illustrates responsible hermeneutics played out in both the teachers' learning and the students' learning. Instead of seeing the Bible as a source of timeless, de-contextualised propositions to be used as knock-down proofs, as the design of the exam questions seemed to convey, it was treated, as N.T. Wright suggested, as a narrative where careful work was required to uncover the meaning and significance for a modern day context in a process where students and teacher were required to reflect on their own pre-understandings and their impact on the interpretation process. That, I suggest, is what we should understand by Christian learning. This is a hermeneutical process of dialogue between text and context and not the extraction of concrete truths for the purposes of transmission and persuasion. Christian learning is learning to be a wise interpreter of an authoritative Scripture.

Conclusion
Too often learning is conceived of by theologically conservative Christians as a process of receiving and applying objective truths found in the Christian's handbook for life, the Bible. Unfortunately, the evidence is that this understanding of learning is unsatisfactory. The case of Tim Farron illustrates the negative experience of many conservatives Christians who think in this way. Some scholars therefore argue that conservative approaches should be abandoned because of the harm they inflict.

---

67 See https://www.bbc.co.uk/news/uk-england-19341722

There is however another way of thinking about Christian learning that is faithful to the conservative understanding of Scripture as authoritative. This draws on the work of a number of leading theologians who have reflected on the relationship between the biblical text and the learner. I have chosen to adopt Anthony Thiselton's designation *responsible hermeneutics* for this process. This emphasises the importance of taking account of one's own pre-understandings in how one learns from the text and of distinguishing between the intended meaning of scriptural passages and the contextually-appropriate significances of that meaning. It also upgrades the attention given to narrative alongside that given to propositions. Understanding learning as a process of responsible hermeneutics allows teachers to embrace the pedagogical priority in their professional work. Learning then is neither just passive reception nor just self-authoring, but self-authoring whilst respecting the framing (and constraining) authority of the biblical text in the creative and critical search for contextually appropriate significances. Such learning accepts that diversity of interpretation is a legitimate outcome of learning and that this means that controversial discussions are a legitimate outcome of biblically faithful learning. Christian learning is not, therefore, a process of baton exchange, but is rather creative living in dialogue with the authoritative biblical text. Had Tim Farron experienced such an approach to Christian learning he would have hopefully felt better equipped to campaign for the PM post in a manner that would have made the Pope proud!

4. "So that they shall not be like their fathers ..." Traditioning and the Limits of the "Formation" Discourse

BERND WANNENWETSCH

"Formation" as schema: the glasses that we don't see as we see through them

The debate on "formation" – whether moral, educational, or political – that in its current form was triggered by the resurgent Aristotelianism that social philosophers like Alasdair MacIntyre[1] have made prominent from the nineteen eighties, has become a formidable success story. "Formation" appears to have become more than a debate and risen to the status of a paradigm. When an idea or a concept becomes paradigmatic, it becomes overly visible – something like a big shadow figure that demands to be taken into account alongside any other concept that comes under review; at the same time, though, it becomes also invisible. A paradigm acts as a framework of thought within which we operate but which itself becomes less and less visible: as when we look through a pair of glasses and over time learn to forget that these frames determine the extent and way in which we see the world.

In that sense, we might say that paradigms of debate are modern forms of what the Apostle Paul called of the "schemata of this age". "Do not be conformed to the schemata of this *aion*", Paul, summons his readers, "but let yourselves be transformed through the renewal of your sense of perception (nous) so that you can discern the will of God" (Rom. 12:2 ...")[2]: The Apostle's call to vigilance over against every paradigm of thought and practice that determines perception in our time, has less to do with the substance than with the efficient form of such paradigms: no

---
1 MacIntyre, Alasdair. *After virtue*. A&C Black, 2013.
2 Translation my own, with particular emphasis on the grammatical use of the medial-passive voice in the Greek. All other quotations from Scripture are taken from the Revised Standard Version.

schema, whether heathen, secular, or even Christian should be allowed to take captive our minds and souls, where that freedom is to rule instead, which is the hallmark of the Holy Spirit. The more successful and paradigmatic an idea becomes, the more vigilant and critical we are to become and make special efforts to prevent ourselves from ending up in a framework of thought, outside of which we cannot think anymore.

What I wish to offer in this contribution is to try and see what insights might arise when reading "formation" as a schema of our age, borrowing from the freedom of the Spirit to think outside the framework of this paradigm and possibly discover viable alternatives to it. For an exercise of this kind, it might be helpful and permissible to operate with a lens that allows for rather sharp contrast. Before we do so, we need to remind ourselves that the success of the "formation" paradigm has had to do with its value in addressing a real problem. "Formation" was not a fancy product of the over-imaginative mind of an intellectual "influencer", populating as it were, the very space that this mind created in the first place. Rather, the "formation" discourse has responded to a real need, resulting from the gap that a substantially thinned out liberalism had created – a liberalism which has cut itself loose from the substantial traditions that made it possible in the first place, leaving behind a vacuum of substantial convictions, values and means of social cohesion.[3]

To this situation, the discourse on "virtue", "character", and "formation", offered a genuine and – most importantly – practically viable alternative. The "formation" discourse has become paradigmatic for one main and simple reason: it works. Empirical viability has always been the strength of Aristotelian types of social and moral philosophy, and the return of virtue ethics has since offered ample proof of this capacity. After *After Virtue*, many discovered how versatile virtue theory was and how well it lent itself to making a career by testing its applicability in an ever-growing scope of academic compartments, with particular emphasis in education and ethics: "a virtue approach to … " – you fill in the blank.[4] Ironically,

---

[3] Bellah, Robert N., et al. *Habits of the heart, with a new preface: Individualism and commitment in American life*. Univ of California Press, 2007; Mulhall, Stephen. *Liberals and communitarians* (1996). Deneen, Patrick J. *Why liberalism failed*. Yale University Press, 2019.

[4] Sandler, Ronald L. *Character and environment: A virtue-oriented approach to environmental ethics*. Columbia University Press, 2009; Gardiner, Peter. "A virtue ethics approach to moral dilemmas in medicine". *Journal of Medical Ethics* 29.5 (2003): 297-302; Moore, Geoff. "Humanizing business: A modern virtue ethics approach". *Business ethics quarterly* (2005): 237-255; Murphy, Patrick E., Gene R. Laczniak, and Graham

the assumed universal viability of the "virtue and formation" approach has effectively contributed to a further departmentalising of ethics, in contradiction to the spirit of its Aristotelian roots, according to which virtue was to be understood politically, as the lifeblood of the polis, tying together every domain of life within it. Nowadays it seems that "virtue" and the "formation" approach associated with it can be transported anywhere and everywhere without loss, as it appears adaptable to business strategies, corporate identity schemes, educational strategies, and – hurrah – also to the Church. If it works everywhere, why should it not also work for theology and Christian Ethics?[5]

To theologians like Stanley Hauerwas, who had worked next door to MacIntyre while the two were colleagues at Notre Dame in the nineteen eighties, the renaissance of "virtue" and "formation" seemed welcome at first, since it put aspects and themes back on the agenda of theologians that had been forgotten or marginalized during the reign of liberal theology: sanctification, the communal, even political nature of the church, the decisive role of character forming sources in Christianity such as the biblical story and ritual practices in worship.[6] Yet, over the years, Hauerwas himself has become more outspoken about the ambiguous nature of this adoption.[7] In accord with his understanding of theology as a polemical discourse that is to keep a vigilant eye on hypotrophies as well as on forgetfulness as critical markers of debates, he has come to understand his making use of "virtue" and "character formation" as an intellectual tool that was useful at one time in order to

---

Wood. "An ethical basis for relationship marketing: a virtue ethics perspective." *European journal of marketing* (2007); Keown, Damien. "Buddhism and ecology: A virtue ethics approach." *Contemporary Buddhism* 8.2 (2007): 97-112; Chan, David K. *Beyond just war: A virtue ethics approach*. Palgrave Macmillan, 2012; Holland, Stephen. "The virtue ethics approach to bioethics." *Bioethics* 25.4 (2011): 192-201.

5 Kotva Jr, Joseph J. *The Christian case for virtue ethics*. Georgetown University Press, 1996; Woodill, Joseph. *The fellowship of life: Virtue ethics and Orthodox Christianity*. Georgetown University Press, 1998; Moore, Geoff. "Churches as organisations: Towards a virtue ecclesiology for today." *International journal for the Study of the Christian Church* 11.1 (2011): 45-65; Fitzmaurice, John. *Virtue ecclesiology: An exploration in the good church*. Routledge, 2017.

6 Hauerwas, Stanley. *Vision and virtue: Essays in Christian ethical reflection* (1986).

7 Hauerwas, Stanley, and Charles Robert Pinches. *Christians among the virtues: Theological conversations with ancient and modern ethics*. University of Notre Dame Press, 1997.

fill a vacuum but that should not be seen as a theory to which theologians should be married to in perpetuity.[8]

An alternative paradigm: traditioning

While we are to appreciate the merits of the "formation" discourse, as it has been shaped by the renewed interest in concepts such as "virtue", "character" and "community", in what follows, I would like to investigate the theological limits and temptations of that discourse when seen from the angle of Israel and the Church. In this perspective, a different paradigm comes to the fore, which for lack of a better term we may call "traditioning".

While the expression may strike us as an Americanism (turning, as it does, a noun into a verbal expression), it is one that actually renders the original meaning of the Latin notion of *traditio* rather faithfully, since it refers less to a deposit of wisdom than to an active process of handing over that wisdom from one generation to the next. In New Testament Greek, there are technical terms for both ends of this process: *paradidonai* (handing over) and *paralambanein* (receiving), as exemplified in the famous expression in 1 Cor. 15, where Paul introduces his summative rendering of the Christian belief in resurrection: "... for I delivered to you as of first importance what I also received, that Christ died for our sins in accordance with the scriptures ..."(v. 3).

So far, so close to the discourse of "formation", we might concede, as the intention inherent in the process of *traditio* is certainly no less a "becoming" of the whole person than it is in character building (*hexis*) of the Aristotelian type. In either case, there is a generation that wishes to induct their offspring to the good and healthy ways of living that they have found constitutive for their own lives and for their identity as a community: how to found a family, to make a home, to make a living, to become a valued and responsible member of society, a good wife, a good father, a good citizen, and so on: all the good things and insights that we can and should adopt from our parents – including the lessons they had to learn the hard way.

Yet, for all those similarities, "traditioning" and "formation" are not the same thing, and the difference is not exhausted by reference to their respective Hebrew and Greek ancestry. Taking a cue from the preposition "*para*" (which means "next to", but can also be rendered "against") that

---

[8] Hauerwas, Stanley. "A retrospective assessment of an 'Ethics of Character.'" *The Hauerwas reader* (2001), 75-89.

governs both technical terms used in NT Greek for describing the process of *traditio*: *paralambanein* and *paradosis*, Hans G. Ulrich has pointed out that *traditio* is "not a mere handing over, passing on, but a giving which runs counter to and is critical of the mere continuation of ways and practices."[9] Rather, as he puts it: "In the process of *traditio* there happens anew the receiving, the adopting and testing for each new generation."[10] This process is both different from and richer than a mere "re-application" of traditional content. With Ulrich's characterizing of *traditio* in mind, we should be better equipped to understand a most perplexing biblical expression that we encounter in the context of the exhortation to traditioning.

"Not like their fathers": liberating discontinuity
Especially in the book of Deuteronomy (6:7) and in the Psalter, the children of Israel are regularly summoned to induct their children to the grand narrative of God's ways with his people, to help them find their place in this story, to learn to live their lives as true Israelites who learn from their fathers and, we would assume, become more like them. But now listen to the actual wording in Psalm 78: 3-8: "Things that we have heard and known, that our fathers have told us ...we will not hide them from their children, but tell to the coming generation the glorious deeds of the Lord ... that the next generation might know them ... and arise and tell them to their children ... so that they should set their hope in God ... keep the commandments and that they should *not* be like their fathers ..."
It is all too easy when reading these verses and getting into their flow to miss out on the small but decisive word that I highlighted in the text: "not". This negation is easy to overlook, as the consecutive logic we are accustomed to read into the flow of passages like this is likely to be quite the opposite: Let us engage in the process of instructing our young ones and the coming generations in the ways that we ourselves have learned as trustworthy and wholesome so that our children may become like us.

---

9 ...dass Tradition "nicht nur Übergabe, Weitergabe, sondern gegenläufige, querlaufende Gabe [ist], wie das griechische Wort ‚paradosis' anzeigt. *Was* weitergegeben wird, steht 'para'– entgegen und quer zu dem, was nur weitergeht oder fortgesetzt wird." Ulrich, Hans G. *Wie Geschöpfe leben*, 2005, 200.

10 "Im Vorgang der *traditio* geschieht erneut das Empfangen, das Aufnehmen und selbst Erproben. Dahinter bleibt diejenige – weithin wirksame – Beschreibung einer Hermeneutik zurück, die ihr die Aufgabe zuweist, 'Traditionsbestände' für eine 'Aneignung' aufzubereiten. Hier wird verdeckt, was in der *traditio* das lebendige Wort ausmacht, was die *paradosis* ist." Ulrich, Hans G. *Wie Geschöpfe leben*, 2005, 344.

This is, indeed, the consecutive logic of "social formation" – the civic logic that we have learned to embrace but which the Psalmist provocatively undermines by saying that the efforts of the parental generation to instruct their children are to culminate in the effect "that they should *not* be like their fathers, a stubborn and rebellious generation."

We might wish to soften that blow by pointing out that our Psalmist must have specifically targeted this disconcerting consecutive phrase at one particular generation: those amongst the "fathers" who actively proved to be a particularly "stubborn and rebellious generation" – like the generation that Moses led through the desert, whose habit of putting serial motions of mistrust against God have become legendary. When reading Psalm 78 at length, we might at first be tempted to think along those very lines, since the Psalmist actually engages a poetic narrative of Israel's desert period including the numerous instances in which this particular generation proved to be "stubborn and rebellious".

Yet the Psalm's narrative does not stop at describing Israel by its desert generation but continues by highlighting the same trait of the people's character when narrating the period after their taking possession of the promised land. Even when a new generation came about that received what God had promised their parents, "they tested and rebelled against the Most High God, and did not observe his testimonies, but turned away and acted treacherously like their fathers; they twisted like a deceitful bow" (vv. 56-57). The Psalmist continues to tell the tale of the people's constant rebellion in contrast to God's constant faithfulness up to the times of King David's reign, the period from which the generation that built the second temple and collated the psalms towards becoming the songbook of Israel took its inspiration

Bearing in mind the wide generational angle that the Psalmist chose and the fact that the psalms in general were (meant to be) sung by every further generation, it appears safe to assume that the disconcerting consecutive twist "that they should *not* be like their fathers", which the psalmist adds to his exhortation to induct the oncoming generations in Israel into the tradition, is not reducible to any particular "stubborn and rebellious generation" in time, but instead must be understood as expressing the logic of what "traditioning" means for the people of God at any time.

A different frame of reference: not polis but torah
As we have seen, for Israel, traditioning is *not* a smooth initiation into the ways and practices of any parental generation; it is not a means to make

any new generation conform to the standards of the society their parents have created. In this biblical point of resistance lies a categorical difference from the Aristotelian notion of "formation". For the Attic philosopher, the frame of reference for becoming virtuous was the Greek city-state, the polis, as reflected in the fact that Aristotle's "Ethics" was part of his "Politics". The core difference from the "not-quite-formation" in Israel that we termed "traditioning" becomes clear when looking at the rather different ways in which the respective communities at stake determine the frame of reference for the processes: "formation" on the one hand and "traditioning" on the other. For Aristotle, the *polis* provides both frame of reference and *telos* for the process of formation. For him, every virtue is by definition a "civic virtue", as defined by a dual constitutive relationship with the polis: these virtues are what it takes for the polis to exist and continue to exist; and it is the polis, which, in turn, gives meaning to any virtue in the first place.[11] Since for the social animals that humans are, any idea of an individual "flourishing life" (as which *arete* can also be rendered) remains meaningless unless embedded within an account of the flourishing of the community to which the individual citizen belongs.

This is why, for Aristotle, the process of "formation", the acquisition of virtues and the developing of character, depends on the actual hierarchy of values in the polis, as expressed in its legislation and codes of honour. The latter in particular allows for a singling out of the most honourable and hence virtuous members – those that are deemed worthy to be taken as examples of a virtuous life, as they are capable of stimulating the mimetic impulses in those that wish to learn how to become virtuous for themselves.[12]

In comparison with the Aristotelian account of formation, when looked at with specific attention given to the constitutive role that the polis plays as a frame of reference that determines both the meaning and *telos* of the virtuous life, the difference that the "traditioning" account in Israel makes becomes rather obvious. The "ways" into which the children of Israel are to be inducted are not simply and directly the ways of the people, but the ways of the torah. It is true that the "fathers" (and mothers)

---

[11] MacIntyre, Alasdair. "The Return to Virtue Ethics." *The Twentieth Anniversary of Vatican II: A Look Back and A Look Ahead: Proceedings of the Ninth Bishops' Conference.* 1990.

[12] Hauerwas, Stanley, and Charles Robert Pinches. *Christians among the virtues: Theological conversations with ancient and modern ethics.* University of Notre Dame Press, 1997.

in Israel are assumed and summoned to be active agents in this process; but their role is structurally different from that of the exemplary representatives of virtue in the polis. The children of Israel are to learn not only *from* their parents directly – learning, as it were, *their* ways –, but also and most importantly, to learn *through* their parents, including the "not-their-ways": the decisive point of difference, which becomes accessible if the children are allowed to see the harmony or contrast of their parents' ways with the "way" that is the torah[13]: *verbum externum*, the alien word of God.

As Psalm 78 has shown us: For children in Israel, their parental generations are to act as witnesses of God's mighty word and deeds that we call the tradition of Israel that alone can instruct them in the ways of the elect people. It is precisely this critical relation between God's word and the ways of those that are to transmit it to the coming generations, which marks the core difference between "traditioning" in Israel and "formation" in Athens. Where Israel has the torah as an *external* framework of reference – since the Word of God can never be owned and exhaustively incorporated into the social body, irrespective of its capacity to "dwell" in the hearts of the faithful –, for Aristotle, the polis is itself the very point of reference for the process of formation and for determining the logic of social or civic formation in principle.

As Stanley Hauerwas and Charles Pinches have demonstrated, following Jean Bethke-Elshtain, the self-referential (and hence potentially totalising) status of the polis as the sole determining factor for the formation of virtues and character in Aristotle's account is particularly apparent in the fact that these virtues are "armed".[14] It is hardly accidental that for Aristotle, in the case of the core virtue of "courage", the exemplar to mimic is the warrior who bravely embraces death on the battlefield. This is so not only because it is only the polis which is worth dying for, but also because it is only the polis which can give meaning to an individual's life, as demonstrated by public rituals of honouring its most valuable members, aimed at securing the everlasting memory of those who courageously died on the battlefield as the truest exemplars of the core virtue of courage. John Milbank has taken this portrayal of the "armed"

---

13 Wannenwetsch, Bernd. "Explorer le champ moral à la Lumière des Commandements de Dieu. Walking the Torah". *Revue des sciences religieuses* 82/3 (2008): 371-387.

14 Hauerwas, Stanley, and Charles Robert Pinches. *Christians among the virtues: Theological conversations with ancient and modern ethics*. University of Notre Dame Press, 1997, 150-151.

nature of virtue a step further by pointing out that any (account of) moral virtue is per definition characterised by its "reactive" character. According to Milbank, any virtue presupposes, dwells on and secretly venerates a specific evil that it aims at overcoming, whether scarcity, death or any other type of a "given" threat to human life and communal flourishing.[15] Milbank contrasts the reactive and inherently violent logic of moral virtue and the ontology of scarcity that it presupposes with the Christian ethics of surplus, receiving and giving in charity, which dwells on a rival (biblical) ontology of surplus that reflects God's being and the operational mode of the Holy Spirit.

Formation in the sense of social conditioning is always centered around an ideal, whether domestic, economic or political: the good husband, the good girl, the good carpenter, the good citizens; to be "good" in this sense means to meet the standard of what fits in neatly and smoothly in a society: of what is useful and consolidating. We gain a healthy suspicion of the idea that this account and type of social "formation" is applicable to the Christian life, when we ask whether there can be such a thing as a "good Christian". By what standards would we measure this quality: with a benchmark for successful ecclesiastical formation?

Christo-formation vs. ecclesial socialisation
At this point, we might recall Dietrich Bonhoeffer's quarrel with the notion of formation (*Gestaltung*) in his "Ethics". The concept "arouses suspicion" for the theologian, as he sees it associated with tiring programs of social engineering that try to impress their own stamp on reality. In contrast to any such idealist construal, for Bonhoeffer, the only formation that has biblical meaning is "being drawn into the form of Jesus Christ."[16] As for the difference between Christo-formation and ecclesial-formation, *kirchliche Sozialisation*, we can assume that for Bonhoeffer, the latter would fall under the same verdict, by which he distanced Christo-formation from programs of social engineering, since the same spirit of idealism[17] that drives the one can also take captive the other: when people are made to conform to ideals of a church life that often are more reflective of standards of decency and class distinction than of the life-giving gospel of Jesus Christ.

---

15 Milbank, John. "Can Morality Be Christian?" *Studies in Christian ethics* 8.1 (1995): 45-59.
16 Bonhoeffer, Dietrich. *Ethics*, DBW 6, 92-93.
17 Bonhoeffer, Dietrich. *Life Together*, DBW 5, 38-47.

If Christo-formation is the ultimate end of the Christian life, what is the *finis proximus* of the biblical concept of traditioning that we contrasted to concepts of social formation and conditioning? The immediate aim of the process of traditioning is clearly stated in the passage from Psalm 78 that we quoted above: "... so that they should set their hope in God, and not forget the works of God" (v.7). We may perceive here an echo of the first Commandment, when the people of Israel are summoned to putting their hope in God and not in other things or other gods. Put their hopes in God, and in God alone, means to be set free from the erratic desires that seek to anchor hope in this or that power, promisemaker, or simply in the sense of belonging and safety that comes with social conformity.

In any case, hope is a power of conforming. In Ps. 135, Israel's God is set in opposition to the fabricated gods of their neigbors. These gods are quite litterally fabricated idols of silver and gold and hence senusally impaired: "They have eyes, but do not see; they have ears, but do not hear" (v. 17). But the challenging conclusion is still to come: those who worship such gods will become like the gods they fabricate, precisely as they are setting their hopes in them. "Those who make them become like them, so do all who set their hope in them" (v. 18).

Without the process of traditioning that allows any new generation to set their hope in the God whom they get to know in the biblical narratives, people are subject to the vagrant desires that the conforming powers (which Paul in Rom. 12:2 calls "schemata") of our age are keen to prey on. "*Me syschematizesthe*": do not be conformed to the schemata of this *aion*, Paul summons the Christian believers, "but be transformed by the renewal of your senses (*aisthesis*)". To understand the difference between traditioning and social formation / conditioning and the corresponding difference between being ruled by the spirit (Gal. 5:18)[18] from either self-governing or being governed by manipulative and exploiting powers, will become all the more important as we appear to be heading into an age of unprecedented social control and conformity, in which we voluntarily hand over control of our lives to the anonymous reign of algorithms for a bit of convenience and a sense of social belonging.

Formation vs. traditioning and formation as traditioning

If the contrast between a pedagogy or ethics of "formation" on the one hand, and that of "traditioning", on the other, has become intelligible and

---

[18] Wannenwetsch, Bernd. "'Ruled By the Spirit': Hans Ulrich's Understanding of Political Existence." *Studies in Christian ethics* 20.2 (2007): 257-272.

– at least in principle – plausible thus far, a question that might present itself at this point is whether this contrast is dependent on the paradigms I have used to define and characterize each account. In particular, we might ask this question with the church in mind.

Even if it seems agreeable that our calling in this case is to follow Israel's lead rather than Aristotle's, the question might arise as to what extent any account of formation must be Aristotelian. The point that I am trying to make is not that every account of "formation" must be Aristotelian in principle, but rather to press the question as to what extent any account of "formation" that presents itself within the ecclesial context reflects the point within the Aristotelian account that I marked as most critical: to make the community and its sanctioned patterns of conduct the sole or determining point of reference for the formational process, so that social formation comes to approximate social engineering.

Everybody is – at least to a significant extent – subject to processes of social formation but not many, especially in Western liberal societies, are traditioned. There is also a degree in which many would attest that ecclesial formation has been part of their social formation. Wherever this is the case, it can and should be embraced with gratitude, but not uncritically. The critical question that we should have gained by now is as to whether such ecclesial formation is (and is content to be) mere formation or whether it is one that extends itself to encompass characteristics that we described as representing the logic of traditioning; whether it contents itself with introducing any new generation to the value system that the church upholds, its doctrinal, moral and cultural standards, or whether "formation" also aims at equipping new generations with what it takes to be traditioned: that along with the "ways" of the fathers – traditions in the plural in the sense of deposits of wisdom that can be handed over -, they are also inducted into ways of subjecting these traditions to the *verbum externum* as their wider and critical framework of reference.

So what, then, is the relation between formation and traditioning? It turns out that we cannot put it in one simple formula: formation and traditioning are neither identical nor opposites. We rather have to assume a complex relationship that suggests a particular order in which to view the matter, just as we have followed it in our procedure thus far: first traditioning vs. formation, then formation as traditioning. In a first step, we had to contrast the two accounts in order to draw attention to a structural difference that cuts right to the core of the respective accounts: where the "formation" logic follows a natural inclination to make the community the sole or predominant point of reference to ensure that any new generation becomes like their fathers, "traditioning" insists on an external frame of reference – the torah or, for Christians, the gospel – as a critical foil that allows the new generations to live truthfully and faithfully "not like their fathers, a rebellious and unfaithful generations".

When and only when this critical point of *structural* contrast is understood and acknowledged, the positive relationship between "formation" and "traditioning" can be addressed and embraced. In this second step we can acknowledge that "traditioning" *materially* dwells in many ways on processes that we associate with social formation. In particular, these will include repetition and ritual, embedded in celebratory and institutional contexts in which these patterns of instruction find their pinnacle expressions.

"Formation as traditioning" will also include making use of personal exemplars that stimulate and orientate the process of personal growth in faith and love. This context is particularly instructive, as it helps us see, once again, that the appreciation of the positive relation of both concepts (formation *as* traditioning) depends on an on-going sensitivity for their critical relation. Within a culture of venerating moral exemplars, the difference between social formation and traditioning will become apparent when it comes to the issue of selecting candidates (who is to be counted amongst those who lead or have led exemplary lives?) and of determining the way in which such lives are presented.

"Social formation" would typically confine that range of candidates to actual or past members of the respective community itself, whereas "traditioning" will make room for sympathetic-critical "outsiders" from whom we can learn as well. It is hence not incidental that the range of exemplars presented in the Bible is as wide as to include a number of outsiders, non-Israelites such as Ruth even included in the messianic ancestry (Matt.1:5), the Samaritan in Jesus' parable (Luke 10), or even a political enemy like the Roman officer who is reported as the first person to publically attest Jesus' divine sonship (Mark 15: 39). One would be hard pressed, in contrast, to imagine Aristotle's polis to include, say, the odd Spartan hero in any of their steles of honour.

Different types of moral exemplars

The inclusion of Rahab in the list of ancestors of the biblical Messiah indicates another characteristic of the Bible's way of dealing with exemplary lives that we can understand as, once again, reflecting the difference between "formation" and "traditioning". The fact that Rahab is included in this list irrespective of her morally dubious profession, demonstrates an account of exemplarity that does not appear to be interested at setting before the reader a picture of a flawless life, lived in moral purity and perfection as perfect example of a character worth to be emulated – as would be expected of heroes and saints in the context of (civil or religious) formation.[19]

Rather, the sober and sometimes painfully realistic biblical portrayal of exemplary people like king David instruct its readers that what is worth emulating in the lives of these persons is not moral perfection but precisely the way in which they deal with their imperfection – when confronted with the divine word that reveals the truth about themselves to themselves. For example, when David was tricked by Nathan into becoming judge of his own adulterous and plotting actions (2 Sam. 12), the king did not react to his being convicted as one might expect – by enacting his royal power to free himself of the nuisance that the prophet must have meant to him (just as King Herod later handled John the Baptist); in contrast to this, the biblical narrative lets the reader know that same adulterous and plotting king allowed the divine judgment against his own self to stand, leading to his contrition, confession and acceptance of punishment.

David in this story is hence a perfect example of the type that the children of Israel are to understand as worth emulating: not in the sense

---

19 It was precisely this characteristic of presenting moral and spiritual exemplars as flawless that caused Martin Luther to be sceptical of the merit of collections like the *legenda aurea* that were more popular in the Medieval Ages than the Bible. In the Reformer's view, such presentations of the lives of saints and their good works as perfect moral exemplars destined for emulation by the common reader were either futile – as their perfection could only instil a sense of unattainability – or hypocritical. In lieu of such books and the "mute" perfection of their protagonist, Luther commended the biblical saints such as presented in the Psalter precisely on the basis that they could function as real human exemplars, based on the transparency of their actions towards their words and hearts. From his Preface to the Psalter (1531): "But above all, there is a virtue and a soul which breathes throughout the Psalms, whilst in other religious books they are full, not of the words, but of the works of the saints. The Psalms are an exception. They breathe the very odour of sanctity: for they not only relate the works but the words of holy men, how they communed with and prayed to God, and how they still commune and pray to him. So that other legends and other examples, when placed in comparison with the Psalms, appear dumb, empty, and unprofitable. The Psalms represent to us the life and the image of sanctity... By these means, we have not only laid open to us their words and their works, but their very heart — the vital treasure of the soul, — so that we can look into the ground and foundation of their words and works, that is into their hearts."

of imitating every aspect of their behaviour but by taking inspiration from those patterns of their action that reflect their willingness to be confronted, convicted and renewed by the divine word as the ultimate critic of their lives. This tripartite structure that reckons with three distinct causes of action – the one who is meant to emulate, the one that is meant to be emulated, and the divine word that critically mediates that emulation – is the hallmark of what we described as "formation as traditioning". Mere formation, by comparison, would be marked by a merely dual account of agency that suggests an unmediated process of emulation in which the exemplar in its own compelling power of moral excellence dictates, as it were, the process as such and in total.

It is true that such formation is not restricted to the two agents as such but always occurs within a particular context and a given frame of reference, such as the antique polis. But the polis or any other comparable cultural or civic context will remain precisely this: "context" that never becomes "text" like the torah, never a living word that assumes its own agency in the process of formation. It is the nature of the living word that "goes out" that "happens" and "never returns empty" and the role it plays in the process of traditioning that helps us understand what is implied positively in the Psalmists statement that "they not become like their fathers". What the new generations should be allowed to experience is not the old – of their fathers' ways –, but quite obviously something new. But how can this "new thing" be understood?

Traditioning and the new thing

Hannah Arendt once famously claimed that education has to be conservative in principle in order for every new generation to be free to bring a new thing into the world.[20] Arendt's statement can certainly be bolstered by the sociological observation that when a generation of parents insisted on being "revolutionary" (as in the student revolt generation of the 1960s) or "forever young", they forced their children into the boring fate of becoming conservative as a reaction. Theologically, though, more is at sake in "traditioning" than an educational conservatism of the type

---

20 "Our hope always hangs on the new which every generation brings; but precisely because we can base our hope only on this, we destroy everything if we so try to control the new that we, the old, can dictate how it will look. Exactly for the sake of what is new and revolutionary in every child, education must be conservative." Arendt, Hannah. "The Crisis in Education", in *Between Past and Future*, enlarged edition, New York, Viking Press 1968, 192-3.

Arendt suggested. What enables a new generation to be genuinely new is not their youth per se or a parental generation's encouragement for them to be different. All too often, the will to be new and original only leads to thinly disguised variations of the old, as in the form of mere inversion.

There is no reason for the Church in particular to buy into the marketing slogan that equates "new" with youthfulness and novelty. The young generation is, of course, important, but not because it is the future of the Church, but because it has a God given right to be instructed in the ways of the future that are tied up with the divine Word as a constant wellspring of renewal. As utterance of the living God who makes all things new, the Word is the true harbinger of the new, and not any new generation by the sheer virtue of being young.

Dietrich Bonhoeffer was particularly sensitive to the way in which the Church is to speak of and relate to what is new. In the introduction to his exposition of Genesis 1-3, he puts it like this: "The Church of Christ witnesses to the end of all things. It lives from the end, it thinks from the end, it acts from the end, it proclaims its message from the end. 'Do not remember the former things or consider the things of old. I am about to do a new thing' (Isa. 43:18-19). The new is the real end of the old; the new, however, is Christ. Christ is the end of the old. Not the continuation, not the goal, the completion in line with the old, but the end and therefore the new. The church speaks within the old world about the new world. ... The old world is not happy to let itself be declared dead. The church has never been surprised by this."[21]

Along these lines, we might say that the main purpose of all Christian proclamation and traditioning is witness to Christ as the truly "new one" and to the Sprit as the only renewer, compared to which the world and its many accelerated metamorphoses remain hopelessly "old" and out of date.[22] It is the ever new appreciation ("not like their fathers") of the ever new-making Word in which an incoming generation will find its calling and challenge. Accordingly, the core task of traditioning on the parental generations' side is to help expose the new generation to that Word which alone can make them new and different in a substantial sense (as opposed to a sense of being different for the sake of being different).

---

21 Bonhoeffer, Dietrich. *Creation and fall: a theological exposition of Genesis 1-3*. Vol. 3. Fortress Press, 1997, 21.

22 Wannenwetsch, Bernd. "Aus Nichts neues Leben zu schaffen ..." Bonhoeffers Anregungen für eine missionarische Kirche im Übergang zur post-christlichen Gesellschaft; in: *Zeitschrift für Dialektische Theologie* 69 (2019), 51-67.

It is important to stress that the Word, although transmitted to the young by their parental generation, remains outside of their parents' control. This word it is not a means of forming the young generation into any image their parents may have conceived in their heads, as commendable or even pious these images might be. Using the word in this fashion – as a tool towards social formation – would turn it into what Paul called (deadening) "letter" as opposed to (live giving) "spirit". In the process of traditioning, however, the word remains *externum*, remains *para*, a word raised "against" all schemes of making humans conform to human expectations and standards[23]. It is the life giving spirit in, with and through the divine Word, acting in the face of any such conforming human law ("letter"), which allows for the newness of life that any new generation should be allowed to embrace and which will make it genuinely "new".

It is in perfect correspondence with this *"para"*-character of the Word that the main form of its proclamation was to be narrative. Narrative is a genre of communication that invites identification – invites, not enforces: the hearers remain free with whom to identify and how. Again, we have a marker of freedom over against social conditioning, which would prioritise rules and principles over narrative.

Non-coercive preaching and a listing heart
Where, then, does our focus on traditioning (vs. social conditioning) make a difference when it comes to concrete practices in which the church lives out its vocation? Towards the conclusion of this essay we must content ourselves with a few hints, to do with proclamation.

In Christian homiletics, a focus on "traditioning" would suggest giving special attention to modes of preaching in which the freedom of the hearer over against the intention of the preacher is maintained – a freedom based on and corresponding with the sovereign freedom of the Spirit. The Spirit alone knows what each individual hearer of the Word and the congregation as a whole need to hear, whether they need to hear a particular word as gospel or law. If the Spirit is, as Luther put it, the sole master of the art of differentiating between gospel and law, restraint must be commended for the preacher to not pre-empt the Spirit's task of

---

23 Hans G. Ulrich speaks of the divine Word as "running counter", as a contradicting word (*widerständiges Wort*). Ulrich, Hans G. "Leben mit Gottes Wort – zur Praxis christlicher Ethik"; in: *Beim Wort nehmen – die Schrift als Zentrum für kirchliches Reden und Gestalten*. M. Krug et. al.(eds), Stuttgart 2004, 196.

differentiation in the process of communicating. In a similar vein, the Apostle Paul's restraint from employing means of irresistible rhetoric in his preaching bears testimony to this difference. "And my speech and my preaching were not with enticing words of man's wisdom, but in demonstration of the Spirit and of power" (1 Cor. 2:4 KJV). In addition to this restraint, the Apostle is keen to stress that what he is to hand on to his congregation is nothing less and nothing more than what he has received (1 Cor. 11:23, 1 Cor. 15:3), the rule of faith which enables his readers to judge for themselves (1 Cor. 14:29), as to whether what Paul or any other preacher is saying is in accordance with this rule, whether it is genuine or a "different gospel". These are all markers of a non-coercive mode of proclamation: the invitation to freely identify with protagonists of the biblical narratives and the invitation to judge any preaching by reference to the rule of faith, instead by reference to any human standard.[24]

So far we have touched upon suitable modes of "handing over" (*paradidonai*) in the process of traditioning, highlighting with Paul the characteristic restraint from using anything that even remotely resembles manipulation and leaving as much operational space as possible for the power of the Spirit. When it comes to identifying, in turn, a mode of perception (*paralambanein*) that is in sync with traditioning, we do so by turning to the biblical motif of the "listening heart" (1 Kings 3:9), the desiring which made young king Solomon count for the wisest of all kings.

In biblical anthropology, the heart is not a muscle that can be trained, formed and brought into shape; rather it is conceived as a non-organ, the free centre of the person – *pars pro toto* – characterizing the directedness and orientation of all sensual and mental human faculties. "Man looks at what is before the eye, but God looks at the heart" (1 Sam. 16:7). The

---

24 "[E]s kann nur darum gehen, dass Gottes Wort gepredigt wird und das Herz frei werden lässt, von dem, was es bestimmt und beherrscht. Mit dieser Predigt, die nur gegen jede Rhetorik gerichtet sein kann, die die Herzen in menschliche Gefangenschaft nimmt, beginnt immer neu die Regierung Gottes – die politische Existenz des Christenmenschen. Was im *Gottesdienst* geschieht, dreht sich um diesen Vorgang. So werden Christen die Bürger der Regierung Gottes, befreit von menschlicher Herrschaft, verborgene Heilige, die keinem Gesetz unterworfen sind und die niemand beherrschen kann. So ist der Christenmensch, der innere Mensch, ein freier Herr aller Dinge und niemandem untertan. Mit dem Gottesdienst als dem Ort dieser Befreiung ist dies eine politische Angelegenheit, die ihre eigene Öffentlichkeit hat, nicht einen *Markt* von Meinungen, Überzeugungen und rhetorischen Strategien." Ulrich, Hans G. *Wie Geschöpfe leben*, 424-25.

Hebrew preposition "le", indicating a direction, suggests that God does not look *into* the heart – like an oversized divine eye penetrating into your inmost secrets – but rather at or even *onto* the heart, in order to see how it is positioned, whether directed towards God and his Word – as a listening heart – or turned elsewhere. In case of the latter, the "heart" will eventually close itself off, become self-referential and "fat" as the Hebrew has it, or "hard" as Jesus puts it (Matt. 19:8). Christ himself is the bringer of the new heart, fulfilling the prophetic promise to replace the heart of stone with a new heart as soft as flesh (Ezek. 36:26) and perceptive to the Spirit. Christ-formation remains the ultimate goal of the Christian life, but the way towards that goal entails a process of formation that we have learned to understand in terms of "traditioning": induction into a way of life, taught by fathers and mothers in faith and in the community of faith, but not as social conditioning but as an allowance for any new generation to find their own "newness" in the life-giving Word as compared to every given instantiation of it in the community.

5. Formation for Ministry. Dilemmas and Perspectives

Hans Schaeffer

Introduction

In this article, I want to provide elements of a heuristic framework that helps us to discover what aspects of theological education are relevant for churches, ministers, and theological training. As will become clear, these elements point to the importance of *liturgical* formation for both future ministers and liturgical practitioners. Such framework and its reflection on theological education and formation have to be connected to both traditions and contexts. This article focuses on aspects of theological education that need elaboration within the context of the Western (Dutch) neo-Calvinist tradition. I start with some initial limitations and definitions.

Contextuality

Any description of formation for ministry is, on the one hand, a very contextual one, but on the other hand, it shares many aspects with some general conceptions of formation. The character and content of formation for ministers depend, for instance, on certain ecclesiological specifics and denominational characteristics of the status of ministers along the spectrum of episcopal-congregationalist. It also depends on the contextual societal positions of churches, on concrete expectations for Christians and Christian institutions within a given society, and on the historical tradition in which an institution of Christian ministerial formation stands – to name just a few explicitly contextual factors. This contributes to the fact that the field of theological education is very diverse by now. Notwithstanding this stress on and need for contextual formation, there are of course supra-local and even global developments that play at least an equal role.[1] The argument in this paper for a specific interpretation of

---

1 Cf. Dietrich Werner et al., eds., *Handbook of Theological Education in World Christianity: Theological Perspectives, Ecumenical Trends, Regional Surveys* (Eugene: Wipf & Stock, 2010).

formation for ministry itself stems from a concrete praxis in a concrete institution for ministerial formation, and yet is also influenced by larger trends in this area.

Definition
We need some initial description of what I mean by 'formation'. In their volume on the relationship between practices and teaching, David Smith and James Smith recall the recent history of Christian education at universities in the context of the USA.[2] Though cultural and educational contexts may differ, it is clear that in societies that are influenced by Western thought, theory (generally spoken) has been privileged above experience or 'practical wisdom'.[3] From a Western perspective, the authors describe both the evident need for Christian research and scholarly involvement in many academic and societal fields, and the need for a Christian pedagogy or 'formation': the training of the workers in all those areas. The former, however, tends to be focused on more at the cost of engaging with the latter, so the authors state, despite the acknowledged need for 'Christian education'. Such education is more than just passing on information. It involves "the spiritual and moral as well as the intellectual formation of students".[4] Discussions about Christian education, however, usually focus on "theological and epistemological frameworks"[5], on the "content"[6] of teaching practices, or on "the personal character or inner self of the teacher".[7] Smith and Smith want to redirect the discussion to the concrete pedagogical practices of Christian formation. Thus understood, learning is about virtues, habits, and practices[8] – and these in the complexity of the many contexts in which we live: school, family, sports, friends, music, etc.. As this article is confined to the formation for *ecclesial ministry*, I focus on a kind of *theological*

---

[2] David I. Smith and James K.A. Smith, eds., *Teaching and Christian Practices: Reshaping Faith and Learning* (Grand Rapids: Eerdmans, 2011).
[3] Cf. for an elaborate overview of this development: Dorothy C. Bass et al., *Christian Practical Wisdom: What It Is, Why It Matters* (Grand Rapids: Eerdmans, 2016).
[4] Smith and Smith, *Teaching and Christian Practices*, 3.
[5] Smith and Smith, 4.
[6] Smith and Smith, 3.
[7] Smith and Smith, 4.
[8] Smith and Smith, 7–11.

education that aims at the formation of virtues, habits and practices of future ministers in the church.[9]

Vocation for Ministry
In order to avoid a quite common misunderstanding regarding any focus on ministers within the life of the church, such focus is not in any way intended to downplay the role of non-ordained ministry or sanctify ordination as some supernatural vocation. I here rely on the simple but helpful distinction the Roman-Catholic theologian Kathleen Cahalan makes in her book *Introducing the Practice of Ministry*. According to her, it is God's overall mission to bring creation back into the life-bringing relationship with Him: Jesus invites us "to become a disciple and to live the life of discipleship".[10] Such life is marked by Christian practices, such as worshipping, witnessing, forgiving, etc., and it is the vocation of any Christian to live such a life. However, it is a specific vocation to become a minister, that is, a distinct vocation "of leading disciples in the life of discipleship for the sake of God's mission in the world".[11] Such vocation is on the one hand a vocation among all the other Christian vocations, whereas it also relates to other vocations in a specific way in that it is concerned with leadership within the Christian community.[12]

Aspects of Formation
Formation for becoming a minister within the Christian community can now be said to entail the spiritual, moral, and intellectual formation of students, aimed at shaping the "hearts and desires"[13] of those who prepare for serving God as a minister within the Church. I want to distinguish three related aspects of this formation that cannot be separated from one another. First, it is about *knowledge*, and acquiring a body of knowledge

---

9 The need for attention to *practical wisdom* in theological education is elaborated further in Hans Schaeffer and Ciska Stark, "Praktische wijsheid en de opleiding tot werker in kerkelijke praktijken," *Handelingen. Tijdschrift voor praktische theologie en religiewetenschap* 48, no. 2 (2021): 21–29.
10 Kathleen A. Cahalan, *Introducing the Practice of Ministry* (Collegeville: Liturgical Press, 2010), 2.
11 Cahalan, 50.
12 Cahalan, 59. "The practices of ministry are distinctive from discipleship as forms of leadership but are deeply connected to discipleship, arising from discipleship for the sake of discipleship".
13 James K.A. Smith, *Desiring the Kingdom: Worship, Worldview, and Cultural Formation* (Grand Rapids: Baker Academic, 2009), 18.

– about God, the Bible, the church, the world, etc. Second, it is also a 'know-how' that allows future ministers to work in and contribute to church practices together with their fellow Christians. This does not only refer to professional skills, but also to something called 'theological interpretation' or *theological reflection*.[14] Formation for ministry comprises of knowledge, of the skill of theological reflection, and – third – of *spiritual formation*.[15] This third element introduces the necessity of explicit talk about God's triune acting within this world in general and in the life of the (future) minister in particular. The Holy Spirit is at work in all of life and in the specific practices of discipleship within the Christian community, and addresses not only the knowledge about God but also the intimate knowledge of God, who is at work in his creation. These three aspects of formation for ministry provide the heuristic framework that bears consequences on the curriculum of theological education. If these three aspects are important, it is clear that formation for ministry is not something for practical-theology alone. It needs integration for the self of the future minister, and that in turn needs integration within the learning context of the theological curriculum.[16] So much for an initial description of what formation for ministry entails.

Outline
The argument of this article is that theological formation for ministry and its institutions need to search for the proper balance between these three

---

14 "The particular knowledge that is unique to ministry is called theological interpretation" – so Cahalan, *Introducing the Practice of Ministry*, 122. Cf. Judith Thompson, *SCM Studyguide to Theological Reflection* (Hymns Ancient and Modern Ltd, 2008); Elaine Graham, Heather Walton, and Francis Ward, *Theological Reflection: Methods* (London: SCM Press, 2005); Bonnie J. Miller-McLemore, *Christian Theology in Practice. Discovering a Discipline* (Grand Rapids: Eerdmans, 2012).

15 Cary Balzer and Rod Reed, eds., *Building a Culture of Faith: University-Wide Partnerships for Spiritual Formation* (Abilene: Abilene Christian University Press, 2012).

16 "Integration is the ongoing process of learning in relation to knowing, being, and doing: each of these aspects of the self is engaged and brought into relationship with each other. Integration is also a goal. It is initiated and formed in and through education but its *telos* is to be a wise and able practitioner. The goal of interpretation for the self relates to ongoing vocational discernment and professional training in which knowledge, practice, and moral commitment become primary ways in which the self is formed" (Kathleen A. Cahalan, "Integration in Theological Education," in *The Wiley Blackwell Companion to Practical Theology*, ed. Bonnie J. Miller-McLemore (Chichester: Wiley-Blackwell, 2014), 389.)

aspects: knowledge, theological reflection, and spiritual formation. To do that concretely, however, in relation to traditions and contexts provides us with several intense dilemmas. In the next section, we will deal with the element of *spiritual formation* as it poses the question of how the necessary stress on spiritual formation relates to the theological principle that we cannot control God's action. The following section deals with the relation between the scholarly, theological side of formation for ministry, and the churchly context in and for which much *theological reflection* takes place. The last element concerns the elaboration of the question of what the body of knowledge in formation for ministry consists of: can we speak about the *what* of theology if we detach it from the *how* of Christian practices. Elaborating on these dilemmas regarding the three aspects of ministerial formation, I point to *liturgical* formation for ministry as a challenging way of dealing with them both contextually and traditionally.

The Theological Dilemma: Spiritual Formation
In this section, we concentrate on the aspect of formation for ministry that highlights the tension between human responsibility and the fact that this formation is not just a human endeavor. Let me start the elaboration of this aspect with Willie James Jennings. In his wonderful book on *The Christian Imagination*, Jennings draws a picture of how Christian faith has consciously and subconsciously led to all kinds of racist opinions and actions by Christians – and not only some badly informed name-Christians.[17] He poses the question, How on earth is it possible that people that are well aware of and even committed to God's great twofold commandment as Jesus says: "Love the Lord your God with all your heart and with all your soul and with all your mind and with all your strength.' The second is this: 'Love your neighbor as yourself.' There is no commandment greater than these." (Mark 12,30-31) – how on earth is it possible that the same people committed to these commandments treat some of their 'neighbors' systematically and pervasively *not* with love? According to Jennings, this has to do with both the lack of and need for reflexive and attentive theological and spiritual formation. Racism is not simply 'bad formation' or (as James Smith calls it) "*mis*-formation of our desires".[18] We need to retell the story of theological formation as a whole in order to provide a theological narration of the origins of race.

---

17 Willie James Jennings, *The Christian Imagination: Theology and the Origins of Race* (New Haven: Yale University Press, 2011).
18 Smith, *Desiring the Kingdom*, 88.

> What is needed, however, is not primarily a historical account of the phenomenon of theology at the *arche* of colonialism (…). [R]ather, theological reflection itself can aid in our analysis of the world that has come upon us. (…) Theology (…) is filled with hope but also analytical, enabling a clearer grasp of the machinations of death and the demonic at work in the world. Theological reflection also opens up the possibility of a conversation that has yet to happen.[19]

Jennings then criticizes theological education. The historical trajectory that shapes the curriculum of most seminaries is concealing the process of "modern identity formation with its constant social performances of detachment, distorting translation, and failed intimacy".[20] We need, says Jennings, to develop an alternative Christian imagination with the attached narrations that leads to an alternative 'social performance of Christianity'. In theological academia, what Jennings observed

> was fundamentally the resistance of theologians to think *theologically* about their identities. It was the negation of a Christian intellectual posture reflective of the central trajectory of the incarnate life of the Son of God, who took on the life of the creature, a life of joining, belonging, connection, and intimacy. Such a posture would inevitably present the likelihood of transformations not only of ways of thinking but of ways of life that require the presence of the risks and vulnerabilities associated with being in the social, cultural, economic, and political position to be transformed.[21]

Jennings clearly makes a plea for theological formation that counters modern, secular formation processes. As such it is an example of what many others within theology have taken up as a great challenge for theology. Theology, as explicit reflection on the Bible, church history, and the dogma of the Church, should be aiming at practicing a salvific way of life by Christians in this world. It should contribute to the formation of a Christian community that fosters true and loving patterns of living together for the glory of God. And this, in turn, points to the formation of ministers that serve such communities, and that serve such fostering. Jennings, therefore, stresses the explicit connection of the theological training and spiritual practices in being real and reflective disciples of

---

19 Jennings, *The Christian Imagination*, 290f.
20 Jennings, 291.
21 Jennings, 7.

Jesus Christ. Theological reflection detached from 'the incarnate life of the Son of God' leads to spiritual distortion, which in turn leads to malpractice.

However, a warning should be given concerning this necessity of spiritual formation as part of theological training, concerning the principal non-manageability of such formation. One that voices such warning is Eugene Peterson. When discussing the necessary prerequisites for doing theology rightly, he calls attention to the subject of spiritual formation in its *passive* nature. "Spirituality is never a subject that we can attend to as a thing-in-itself on our own, but requires formation by God's Spirit, a complex and lifelong way of being. It is always an operation of God the Spirit in which our human lives are pulled into and made participants in the life of God, whether as lovers or rebels".[22] The phrase 'spiritual formation' can easily be misconceived as "projects of self-improvement, the imposition of codes of conduct, and ventures into spiritual technology".[23] Formation should not become "a project that we take over and manage".[24]

So here we have the first dilemma that is attached to 'formation for ministry'. How should we conceive of such formation in both its utmost necessity and its principal non-manageability? Necessity, because the neglect of conscious formation leads to dangerous distortions of the very essence of God's salvific actions, and non-manageability because it is principally not something we can somehow achieve or bring about as a 'good' inherent to human practices. This might be called the *theological dilemma*. Theologically speaking, one of the most important and recurring themes is about the distinction and connection between God and creation.

The Ecclesial Dilemma: Theological Reflection
There is, however, a second dilemma that needs our attention. Training students for ministry involves some kind of hermeneutical awareness, the attitude needed to become 'reflective practitioners'.[25] Such reflection, however, always bears the tension between a primary context, i.e. church

---

22 Eugene Peterson, "Spirituality/Spiritual Formation," in *Dictionary for Theological Interpretation of the Bible*, ed. Kevin J. Vanhoozer (Baker Academic, 2005), 768.
23 Ibid.
24 Peterson, "Spirituality/Spiritual Formation," 769.
25 Cf. e.g. Donald Schön, *Educating the Reflective Practitioner toward a New Design for Teaching and Learning in the Professions* (San Francisco: Jossey-Bass, 1987).

practices, and a secondary one, i.e. theological education. Let me elaborate on the possible tensions this distinction creates from one concrete and local example. The theological institution I am serving, Kampen Theological University, stands in the Reformed, and more specifically: neo-Calvinist tradition. This tradition is well known for its attention to theological reflection and education, and has worldwide instances.[26] A provisional list of institutions of theological education from a Reformed perspective is impressive.[27] In this respect, the Reformed tradition greatly differs from, for instance, the Evangelical one. As Richard Mouw says with an understatement: "A strong commitment to theological education cannot be taken for granted in the evangelical community".[28] Mouw, however, being a distinguished Reformed scholar and theologian, comparing the Reformed and Evangelical tradition, eloquently moves into a defense of the standpoint that formal theological training is not necessary, by referring to its theological rationale – a rationale that transcends any confessional rift between Reformed and Evangelical: "[E]ducation has to be subordinate to the religious calling".[29] The vocation of God cannot and must not be confined by theological requirements or training. This existential commitment to faith and to obedience to God is the reason why the tension between theological education and the church is never to be obliterated – even not in the Reformed tradition. In the history of theology at least until the twentieth century, faith in and obedience to God were considered necessary prerequisites for doing theology, as were church commitment and involvement. The training and formation of ministers imply some kind of connection between theology and the Christian community of faith.

Yet theology also distances itself from faith, belief, and church. Theological training also implies critical and conscious reflection on faith practices, of oneself, of other church members, of the church as a whole.

---

26 Lukas Vischer, "Reformed Theological Education and the Unity of the Church," in *Handbook of Theological Education in World Christianity: Theological Perspectives, Ecumenical Trends, Regional Surveys*, ed. Dietrich Werner et al. (Wipf & Stock Pub, 2010), 667–71.

27 Jean Jacques Bauswein and Lukas Vischer, eds., *The Reformed Family Worldwide: A Survey of Reformed Churches, Theological Schools, and International Organizations* (Grand Rapids, Mich: Wm. B. Eerdmans Publishing Company, 1998), 563-699.

28 Richard J. Mouw, "Challenge of Evangelical Theological Education," in *Theological Education in the Evangelical Tradition*, ed. D. G. Hart and R. Albert Mohler (Grand Rapids, Mich: Baker Pub Group, 1996), 284.

29 Mouw, 286.

Lukas Vischer summarizes these two aspects, connection and distance, with the keywords *freedom* and *communion of Christ's church*.[30] Theological education should be able to reflect critically on the teaching of the church, and is not necessarily called to confirm the *status quo*. At the same time, theology itself is a thoroughly Christian practice that takes place within the communion of the church; theologians are often part of church communities, and their training aims at working within communities of faith. Exactly because – in both Evangelical and Reformed thinking – obedience to God is more important than any human endeavor, both critical and loyal theological education is needed. This both-and of theological reflection and connection with communities of faith gives rise to "a double temptation" as Vischer states: "For the church to treat theological schools as simple 'tools' or, for theological schools, to claim entire independence from the life and witness of the church".[31]

Formation for ministry is both intrinsically intertwined with the practices of the church, and yet has to distance itself from it as reflection on those practices. That is the second dilemma, that is present in many institutions around the globe. Just to mention an example from within the neo-Calvinist tradition, I point to an aspect of the history of one of its prominent institutions.[32] This institution of formal theological training dates back to mid-19th-century Reformed church-life when, in the aftermath of a church division, the need for training of ministers of this newly founded denomination resulted in its beginning. Its history of more than 150 years shows a constant back-and-forth between academic

---

30 Vischer, "Reformed Theological Education and the Unity of the Church," 668. He writes this with respect to the task of unifying Reformed churches, but it also captures the condition of Reformed theological education in general.

31 Vischer, 670. Some, like Michael Beintker, try to implement this balance by separating the academic phase of theological education from the ecclesial phase. "Training in two phases has proved itself. It provides the spiritual free space that is necessary for the processes of training if they are to succeed. It relieves academic study of premature evaluations of interest and preserves it from any professional pragmatism which without theological education will ultimately imprison itself in a lack of orientation and burn itself out" (Michael Beintker, "The Study of Protestant Theology in Europe," in *Handbook of Theological Education in World Christianity: Theological Perspectives, Ecumenical Trends, Regional Surveys*, ed. Dietrich Werner et al. (Eugene: Wipf & Stock, 2010), 559.) My question would be, whether such phasing does not (unintentionally) concede to the temptation to separate church and school, rather than really stimulate both to interact.

32 George Harinck and Wim Berkelaar, *Domineesfabriek: geschiedenis van de Theologische Universiteit te Kampen* (Amsterdam: Prometheus, 2018).

and church commitment, intertwined with and closely related to the course of the Reformed Churches that founded (and financially supported) it. The authors clearly do not value church commitment as bad, but they abundantly show that in practice, this has more than once led to blind spots in theological reflection on the life of the church.

One important example of such a blind spot is what the authors notice regarding the theological reflection on the history of the Reformed Churches. Within its own institute for theological training for future ministers, scholarly and scientific *theological* reflection on the confessional and historical stances of the Church was virtually impossible, unless it valued the denomination's history – and especially the crucial choices in times of the major mid-twentieth-century church-split – as 'work of God'. The authors give many examples of how such a position worked out in practice, and what tensions among the teaching staff this created, as not everyone consented to this position.[33] The history of this institution displays the complicated relationship between church and university, faith and reflection.

We might, perhaps, call this the *ecclesial dilemma* of theological education. To what extent have theology and faith, theology and church-life, theology and church-practices to be distinguished from each other?

The Pedagogical Dilemma: Theology as What and How
Any claims about the training for ministry entail definitions of 'theology'. How theology is defined, then, correlates with the framing of the 'how' of theological education. This can be illustrated by referring to another concrete example of Reformed theologians providing an explanation of what *Reformed Theology Today* entails.[34] It defines theology as 'scientific practice in the midst of concrete church life'. This context is highly valued, and this volume is an example of how the ecclesial dilemma of theological

---

33 Harinck and Berkelaar, 250f.304.312-344.393f.400f.423f.489. Especially after the church-split in 1944, the connection between the RCL and their theological institute was so strong: church-members were very loyal to the TUK, and the University on the other hand 'surrendered to' the churches ("Enerzijds versterkte [het sociale isolement sinds de Vrijmaking] de onderlinge band van de vrijgemaakten en ook de trouw aan de opleiding. Nooit in de geschiedenis van de Kamper instelling is ze zo op handen gedragen als door de vrijgemaakten, het meest algemeen in de jaren zeventig. Anderzijds leverde de Universiteit zich in deze periode te zeer aan de kerken uit" (489)).

34 Ad de Bruijne, ed., *Gereformeerde theologie vandaag: oriëntatie en verantwoording* (Barneveld: Vuurbaak, 2004).

education is treated. Theology stands or falls with the spiritual relationship with God, and concrete practices of faith are primary whereas theology is secondary. The object of theological reflection is phrased as 'God in the reality of his revelation; the life of the Christian community in this world; and creation – and these three in their mutual relationships'.[35] Elaborating on the neo-Calvinist tradition of Abraham Kuyper, a division of theology is proposed in six different areas: Bible, history, systematic-theology, and practical theology, along with ethics and missiology.

Theology, thus conceived, is defined by its content: what is the object of theology? Little is said about the 'how' of theological education, some specific academic curriculum – let alone about the content or character of such theological formation. That brings us to the third dilemma: is theology about 'what' is taught, or is it also about the 'how'? Is theology a description of content, or of method? Or, can the 'how' (theological education) be part of the 'what'?

A historical remark is in place here. As the much-praised historian and theologian Justo González has sufficiently shown, the history of theological education has its origins in the catechetical tradition. In early Christianity, there was no professional training of bishops. Neither Augustine nor Ambrose, to name two learned and influential theologians and church leaders of their time, underwent a specific curriculum that prepared them for their ministry. In fact, even in the heyday of medieval theology, only very few parish priests had specific ministerial training.[36] It was not until the Reformation and the Counter-Reformation that specific institutions for theological education were founded, like Luther's reform of the University of Wittenberg and Calvin's *Academie* in Geneva. Gonzáles writes:

---

35 Bruijne, 11.17.
36 "Although historians - particularly those interested in the history of thought and of theology - have paid much attention to the universities and the professors, the fact is that the proportion of clergymen who had university studies was minimal. In spite of the growth of cities, still most of the flock lived in rural areas, where the parish priest was not expected to know much. ... Thus, one frequently finds references to priests who had no more knowledge than what they had learned by heart in order to celebrate the mass and other rites" (Justo L. González, *The History of Theological Education* (Nashville: Abingdon Press, 2015), chap. 8.) When discussing the formation for ministry in the early church, González remarks: "[A]lthough there are many indications that a good number of the bishops of the second century were relatively learned people who at least know how to read, how to interpret texts, and how to sustain a correspondence with their colleagues, there is no indication that the church had any schools for the training of such bishops or pastors" (chap. 1).

Such was the success of these institutions that soon formal theological studies became a requirement for ordination - which had never been the case at any point in the history of the church and would now become the norm for many churches at least until the twenty-first century.[37]

Those new institutions took over the habits of medieval universities. Putting it bluntly: theological training was clothed in scholastic robes that were not always fitting for the work in the parish. In his epochal work on theological education Edward Farley, one of the most important names in the field of theological education, describes how this development led to a twofold distortion of theological education. First, following the developments of the German university in the 18th and 19th centuries, theology evolved into a conglomerate of many specialized subdisciplines. Second, following mostly on Schleiermacher, it took theology to aim at ministerial practices that applied the specialized insights into church life in its leadership role. Farley coined the phrase 'clerical paradigm' to encompass these two flaws of theological education.[38] Farley's view is rightly criticized for its depreciating tone on theology's focus on the praxis of church life, thereby neglecting the perhaps even more pervasive *academic* paradigm as the main cause for distortion.[39] Yet, the debate Farley fueled has led to significant contributions to theological education. Especially within the field of practical theology, it became clear that the mere application of systematic and Biblical truths into practice was not a fruitful scheme. The very nature of theology itself was at stake. We need a coherent, comprehensive view on the formation of the minister's identity, including the concrete pedagogical aspects of it. I would like to take this third dilemma to be the *pedagogical dilemma* of

---

37 González, ch 10.
38 Edward Farley, *Theologia. The Fragmentation and Unity of Theological Education* (Eugene: Wipf & Stock, 1994).
39 Miller-McLemore, *Christian Theology in Practice*, 160-184 ('The Clerical and the Academic Paradigm'); Bonnie J. Miller-McLemore, "Practical Theology and Pedagogy: Embodying Theological Know-How," in *For Life Abundant: Practical Theology, Theological Education, and Christian Ministry*, ed. Dorothy C. Bass and Craig Dykstra (Grand Rapids, Mich: Eerdmans, 2008), 170–90. It was not until 2005 that Farley himself acknowledged the deep influence of the *academic* paradigm which caused him to miss the pedagogical aspect of theological education, cf. Miller-McLemore, *Christian Theology in Practice*, 180. Miller here quotes Edward Farley, "Four Pedagogical Mistakes: A Mea Culpa," *Teaching Theology and Religion* 8, no. 4 (2005): 200–203.

theology. Should theological education be about the 'what' or the 'how' of acquiring theological knowledge?

Within the conceptual framework of Western theology after the Enlightenment, attention to 'how', to the pedagogy of doing theology has not been prominent. It may, however, well be the case that such attention is nowadays framed in terms of 'hermeneutics'. I contend that the Reformed attention to hermeneutics is a very specific, contextual and traditioned way of dealing with the 'how' of theological education. Let me illustrate this by the example of a book called *Reformed Hermeneutics Today*.[40] It can be considered a counterpart of the book on theology from the same specific tradition.[41] The neo-Calvinist tradition and its conception of theology takes God's revelation in general, and the Bible in particular, to be central in Reformed theology. Reflection on how we read the Bible provides a unique entrance into theological education as a specimen of how Christians should read the Bible. As systematic-theologian Hans Burger, one of the editors of this book on hermeneutics, states: reading the Bible is transformative, and therefore 'hermeneutical' and 'spiritual' formation need to go hand in hand.[42] It may very well be the case that attention to 'hermeneutics' here serves as an unconscious answer to the problem of theological education, of the 'how' of doing theology, of the intrinsic need for soteriological premises in doing theology. However, I think we better reflect on the concept of 'formation' instead of hermeneutics to address the important themes involved here.

Liturgical Formation as a Way Out
In the previous sections, we stated that formation for ministry is marked by at least three dilemmas. First, we discussed the theological dilemma:

---

40 Ad de Bruijne and Hans Burger, eds., *Gereformeerde hermeneutiek vandaag: theologische perspectieven* (Barneveld: Vuurbaak, 2017).
41 Bruijne, *Gereformeerde theologie vandaag*.
42 Cf. Hans Burger, "Theologische hermeneutiek in soteriologisch perspectief," in *Gereformeerde hermeneutiek vandaag: theologische perspectieven*, ed. Ad de Bruijne and Hans Burger (Barneveld: Vuurbaak, 2017), 35–65; Hans Burger, "Theologie: een hermeneutisch model," in *Gereformeerde hermeneutiek vandaag: theologische perspectieven*, ed. Ad de Bruijne and Hans Burger (Barneveld: Vuurbaak, 2017), 263–83. I myself contributed to this theme by explaining the importance of formation within practical theology: Hans Schaeffer, "Vorming en normativiteit. De rol van de Schrift in de praktische theologie," in *Gereformeerde hermeneutiek vandaag: theologische perspectieven*, ed. Ad de Bruijne and Hans Burger (Barneveld: Vuurbaak, 2017), 199–217.

spiritual formation is necessary and yet not manageable as the Spirit is not something human beings can control. The second dilemma was the ecclesial one: how can the relation between academic theology and the church be fruitful? Third, we encountered the pedagogical dilemma: how much attention should be given to the 'how' of theological education – especially in the context of the post-Christian, post-Enlightenment context of theological education in the West.

Institutions for theological training need to take these dilemmas seriously. It is my thesis, as I said at the beginning, that *liturgical* formation provides a way to deal with these dilemmas and tensions. Theological training would thus profit from an alignment with great parts of the history of theological education. As we saw earlier, theological education was closely connected to the tradition of the catechumenate.[43] It was training in celebrating the liturgy. However great the differences between localities, cultures, and periods in history may be, liturgy might be the most promising area in which to locate theological education. Liturgical formation for ministry provides the necessary means for explicitly dealing with these dilemmas. I will offer seven reasons for this.

First, as James Smith has shown, liturgy – broadly conceived – captures the notion of human formation *in general*. Though it might sound obvious, it is in fact a strong counter-cultural statement Smith makes, following Augustine, Bourdieu, and Merleau-Ponty. It entails the claim that the typical Enlightenment freedom human beings are supposed to 'have', is always mediated: there is no absolute freedom. We become what we are by participating in formational practices, 'liturgies' as Smith calls them. "[L]iturgies – whether 'sacred' or 'secular' – shape and constitute our identities by forming our most fundamental desires and our most basic attunement to the world. In short, liturgies make us certain kinds of people, and what defines us is what we *love*."[44] This should then better be elaborated upon, in order to prevent such formation from shaping us without reflection. That is why James Smith continues by saying that we need to make explicit, what relation between formation and worldview is envisioned. "[E]very liturgy constitutes a pedagogy that teaches us, in all sorts of precognitive ways, to be a certain kind of person. Hence every liturgy is an education and embedded in every liturgy is an implicit worldview or 'understanding' of the world".[45] Liturgy, then, may be a

---

43 González, *The History of Theological Education*, chap. 2 and 3.
44 Smith, *Desiring the Kingdom*, 25.
45 Smith, 25.

starting point for any education but it certainly may be the primary context of theological education.

Second, liturgy is broader than hermeneutics – most obviously for its encompassing all kinds of experiences and practices that go beyond 'reading the Bible'. It is within the setting of the liturgy that the Bible is read and interpreted. Even the very reformed saying *sola scriptura* cannot be treated apart from its liturgical context.[46] Liturgy provides us with a window back into 'the Church catholic' in the sense of the Apostolic Creed – which, I would say, is important in a world that is so localized and divided into separate bubbles and group identities.

Third, ideally – as opposed to not every but many occasions in reality[47] – liturgy opens up the space in which we on the one hand fully take part in core Christian and faithful practices, and on the other hand, are by that enabled to critically reflect on it. One of the objectives of the liturgy is that it transforms us, not magically but creatively: that is, we believe that God himself works through these Christian practices with the transformative power of the Holy Spirit.

Fourth, starting with liturgy makes it clear that ministerial formation is in a continuum with all Christian formation. It was the rediscovery of the Reformation that by baptism, all Christians are called to a Christian life, which profoundly qualifies the vocation for ministry as just one (albeit specific) vocation within Christian faith. Ministerial formation is needed not because ministers are higher, better, or whatever, but because "ministry is a distinct vocation among many vocations that exist within the Christian community. … The self-identity of the minister is rooted in discipleship and the further deepening of that identity takes place by living the demands of discipleship in and through the vocation to ministry".[48] Especially within a Reformed, post-modern context, this element could not be stressed enough to prevent any unnecessary

---

46 Cf. Hans Schaeffer, "Sola Scriptura and the Formative Role of Practical Theology," in *Sola Scriptura*, ed. Hans Burger, Arnold Huijgen, and Eric Peels (Leiden: Brill, 2017), 294–311.

47 Cf. D.H. Tripp, "Liturgy and Pastoral Service," in *The Study of Liturgy*, ed. Cheslyn Jones et al., 2nd, rev.ed. ed. (London: SPCK, 1992), 567. Tripp writes: "[T]he whole range of events in worship (not just the successes, not only the grace) is part of the history in which the divine and the human act and interact. The description of all this encounter, and of what happens or fails to happen in it, is part of each generation's theological agenda".

48 Cahalan, *Introducing the Practice of Ministry*, 49.

objections against any stress on ministry apart from and over against the community of the church as a whole.[49]

Fifth: starting theological education within the liturgy, on the one hand, provides the necessary embodied, specific, and local context in which and through which (on the other hand) the tradition of the church and its catholicity can be accessed and lived. In a rapidly and vastly changing world, we need to ensure that God's people do not drift away from participating in practices that are acknowledged as their source of freedom. As a report on the present challenges for society in the Netherlands states, we need sustainability and solidarity[50] – the former implying at least some coherent and 'proven' forms of life. Elaborating on 'liturgy' in its formative power provides Christians with a specific and salvific, sustainable, and solidary wellspring of concrete practices which offers rich perspectives for social action as well. Liturgy is one way of preserving sustainable solidarity within the church and widely beyond its formal borders.

Sixth, liturgy is one of richest and most dense practices of Christian faith that immediately bears effect on the Church's place in and for the world. Theological education for ministers that starts in liturgy thus starts not within an obsolete ritual of like-minded hobbyists, but (again, ideally) from within practices that lovingly and critically relate to the whole of God's creation. It provides a fruitful framework for treating ethics, as the work of Hauerwas, Wells, and Wannenwetsch abundantly shows.[51]

Finally, liturgy may be the only context in which we can fruitfully develop the concept of ministry after all. D.H. Tripp remarks in his excellent essay that "all ministry is essentially (not exclusively) liturgical".[52]

---

49 Cf. the chapter on 'Writing the Body of Christ: Corporate Theological Reflection' that says: "Theological reflection in this frame is a corporate activity undertaken in everyday life as ordinary people draw on the traditions of faith, as these are encountered in scripture, worship and life together, in order to make concrete responses to the world in which they live" (Graham, Walton, and Ward, *Theological Reflection*, 128).

50 "De Toekomst Tegemoet - SCP," 2016, https://www.scp.nl/Publicaties/Alle_publicaties/Publicaties_2016/De_toekomst_tegemoet.

51 Bernd Wannenwetsch, *Political Worship: Ethics for Christian Citizens* (Oxford: Oxford University Press, 2004); Stanley Hauerwas and Samuel Wells, eds., *The Blackwell Companion to Christian Ethics*, 1 edition (Malden, Mass.: Wiley-Blackwell, 2006).

52 Tripp, "Liturgy and Pastoral Service," 572. "In education for ministry, in each generation, there has inevitably to take place a renegotiation of educational aims and objectives. Equally pressing is the need for the Church's ministers in mid-career to ask again what they are for, and whether they can find reasons and means to keep going. In both quests, unless the Christian ministry (re)discovers itself in terms of the worshipful God, its enterprise will descend into idolatry or masked atheism" (573).

That is in line with the remarks of former church-polity professor Leo Koffeman. He states that it is the context of the liturgy that qualifies and necessitates ministry: people are gathered upon the calling of God, around Word and sacrament. It is "in the liturgy that the congregation is born," says Koffeman.[53] The congregation, and the minister who is called to serve her, share their origins in the practices of the liturgy, which practices in turn function as the content and way in which Christian life and community take shape. Formation for ministry, therefore, stems from the liturgy. As well as all Christian education is ultimately aimed at serving God as disciples of Jesus, ministry that is called to serve God's community may take the liturgy as its natural habitat and form.

Conclusion

These seven arguments, in which formation for ministry originates from the liturgy of the church, point to the fact that the practices of liturgy itself deal with the three dilemmas mentioned. Liturgy is not just a human endeavor but relies on God's active and mediated engagement in this world, and liturgical formation thus addresses the *theological dilemma* that God's actions and human action are intertwined. Liturgical practice and theological reflection are correlational, as the famous dictum *lex orandi lex credendi* indicates (see Maarten Kater's contribution in this volume). Furthermore, Christians always should reflect critically on what they do, and why, and for what context: the *ecclesial dilemma*. Liturgical formation is a way of concretizing this dilemma by practicing liturgy and reflecting on it. Thirdly, the concept of practice in general, and of liturgical practice in particular, indicates that the pedagogical dilemma is real: the what and the how are codependent. Rather than locating theological training mostly in the academy, the concrete liturgical practice that is at the center of church life offers a concrete and contextual learning environment for future ministers that provides great opportunities in terms of both form and substance for formation for ministry.[54]

---

53 L.J. Koffeman, *In Order to Serve: An Ecumenical Introduction to Church Polity* (Zürich: LIT, 2014), 88. Cf. also Alexander Schmemann, *For the Life of the World: Sacraments and Orthodoxy* (Yonkers: St Vladimir's Seminary Press, 2018); Nicholas Wolterstorff, *The God We Worship: An Exploration of Liturgical Theology* (Grand Rapids: Eerdmans, 2015).

54 For an elaboration on the central position of the liturgy, cf. Hans Schaeffer, *Kerk om te vieren: praktisch-theologische reflecties op kerkzijn* (Kampen: Summum Academic Publications, 2019).

Elaborating on this beyond the scope of this article, I would just say that formal theological training for ministry that takes liturgical practices as its starting point, should of course entail a proper account of liturgical practices. Celebrating the Lord's Supper, for instance, may serve as a rich example of this. It contains initial answers to the three dilemmas mentioned above. It offers rich perspectives on community formation as a work of the Spirit and of human beings, reflecting the theological dilemma of formation as both a spiritual and human endeavor. Celebrating the Lord's Supper involves elements of rich and complex reflection on the individual in relation to the community with respect to all kinds of moral questions like social injustice, social inclusion, personal ethics, etc. Practicing the Lord's Supper, thus, is a form of spiritual formation (the theological dilemma). It also implies that from this formation may proceed critical reflection on how this liturgical practice is done, as the ecclesial dilemma of theological reflection points at. And, finally, taking part in liturgical practices offers the concrete context of reflection on 'how' important theological and practical faith issues can be dealt with, as has been shown for instance in the important *Blackwell Companion to Christian Ethics*.[55] Liturgical formation thus is a promising context for theological formation for ministry that, in turn, may contribute to the concrete transformation of church practices as well.

---

55 Samuel Wells and Stanley M. Hauerwas, *The Blackwell Companion to Christian Ethics*, 2. edition (Malden: Wiley-Blackwell, 2011).

6. Pray what you believe, and believe what you pray

Maarten Kater

Formation in the Church by the 'lex orandi, lex credendi'- Rule (LOLC) from the perspective of Hebrews[1]

Introduction
The fact that a liturgy does something with lives of people is called the formative effect of the liturgy[2]. This applies not only to official worship liturgies, but even to more or less loose 'liturgies' used at home e.g. when a meal is closed by reading the Bible, praying and singing. Even outside such a conscious process of formation there is our daily life as a liturgy which forms the lives of so may people[3]. After all, people receive a lot of formation which is due to what human beings learn by the way, without preconceived intentions. In this chapter, however, we discuss the relation between de above mentioned 'official' liturgy in churches and theology.

This relation between theology and worship is formulated in the well-known and very often cited *lex orandi - lex credendi* rule (LOLC) during the last decades. Quite often – and I will argue that this means *too* often- it is cited in order to say: theology should follow the liturgy, and: prayer is the hermeneutical key to our doctrine of God. But is the LOLC-Rule really meant to say this?

This topic requires a brief further introduction. What in the world does this saying mean: *lex orandi lex credendi* ? As just mentioned, very often this rule is put in this way: what we pray is, ought *to be* and/ or *is, decisive* for the way we believe. A rule that seems to derive from the *lex*

---

[1] This lecture has received another edit in: Maarten Kater & Ferdi Kruger, *Preaching in Arduous Times: Outline of Perspectives from the Hebrews Sermon on Preaching* (Kampen: Summum Academic Publications, 2021).
[2] Nicholas Wolterstorff, *The God we worship: An exploration of liturgical theology* (Grand Rapids: Eerdmans, 2015).
[3] Tish Warren, *Liturgy of the Ordinary. Sacred practices in everyday life* (Downers Grove : Inter Varsity Press, 2019).

orandi follows the *lex credendi*, so the *lex orandi* 'is' the *lex credendi*, and not the other way round. But where is the verb? We'll see that originally there was no verb in this sentence at all. Who has invented or given us this rule? It seems important to know this, because our faith practices are involved, our theologies are involved, and the complete formation by means of education in preaching and catechism classes and by means of pastoral care, are involved in our churches. Fortunately, this rule did not appear out of the blue, although, sometimes, it seems to be used in that way, as though it belongs to the *regula fidei* itself. One could hear a Catholic defend this rule by saying: we must hold fast to a fixed liturgy or otherwise our faith will be diminished. On the other hand, a Protestant embraces the rule in quite another sense: of course we subscribe to this rule (we love), because the congregation is the source for real theology for us; there's no other theology than that occurring from the lived or espoused theology in the church[4]. So this seems to be a rule one can interpret in the way one likes, and that would actually be to say the same as this is no rule at all. And at the end – as we will see in this chapter - it is actually true: there is not a LOLC-rule at all in the sense it is very often used, while the abbreviated version turns out to be just a short-cut of the original intention. Nevertheless, I keep writing about this rule because it is that short version which is in the mind of most people and has obtained a place in many practical theological studies. To put it very briefly, although this rule is historically seen appears to be a monster, from a theological perspective nevertheless it could be useful when thinking about 'education, formation and the church'. Nevertheless, everything depends on how we use it, from which direction we read it as will be shown.

Therefore, after we have explored the current use, as found in section 1 below, we will take a brief historical detour in paragraph 2 because, if we miss the historical information, the formation of this often used rule, we have to be aware of the great danger of another triad 'education, *de*formation and the church'. Once we have thus visited the historical background, we will briefly consider this rule as it is evaluated from the perspective of the letter to the Hebrews in paragraph 3. We take this perspective, because it has played a formative role in Christian theology throughout the centuries and more than any other part of the New Testament the letter is connected with aspects of the worship of God.

---

[4] Helen Cameron, et al, *Talking about God in practice: Theological action research and practical theology* (London: SCM Press, 2004).

Hebrews offers us in the format of a sermon the various aspects of liturgy, and even Jesus Christ is referred to as the Liturgist *par excellance* (Hebr. 8:1).

I will close the chapter with some remarks on the use and misuse of this rule considering such practical-theological phenomena as education and formation in relation to the church.

The linguistic ambiguity
One of the maxims of contemporary liturgical theology has remained the slogan introduced above: *lex orandi, lex credendi* (LOLC). Recently and increasingly scholars have argued that liturgy itself is theology, indeed, primary theology (*theologia prima*) from which is derived all secondary theology (*theologia secunda*), namely subsequent theological reflection on the liturgy[5]. Thus, the liturgy is primary and formulated doctrines are secondary, derivative and subordinate. This notion 'challenges the common Reformed view that liturgy follows theology'[6]. For several decades now, there has been a 'tug-of-war' between liturgical scholars 'over whether liturgy should exercise control over doctrine or doctrine should exercise control over liturgy'[7].

A very short exploration shows us the two main streams in the use of the expression LOLC. This saying is interpreted as *orandi* == > *credendi* by Aidan Kavanagh and David Fagerberg to mean that 'the law of praying (*lex supplicandi* or *lex orandi*) establishes (*statuat*) the law of believing (*legem credendi*)'[8]. Thus, in their view, what is meant by *lex orandi* exists prior to and determines the *lex credendi*, and the latter, therefore, cannot be the foundation of the former. The 'relationship of praying and believing is unidirectional; we do not believe and then worship, but we encounter God in worship, and therefore we believe' (ibid.). The liturgy, then, is primary and establishes theology: the order cannot be reversed. 'Secondary theology, then, as a presentation of belief, follows from worship.'(ibid.).

---

5 David W. Fagerberg, *Theologia Prima: What is liturgical theology?* (Chicago/Mundelein: Hillenbrand Books, 2004), 36-69.
6 Martha L. Moore-Keish, *Do this in remembrance of Me: A ritual approach to Reformed Eucharistic Theology* (Grand Rapids: Eerdmans, 2008), 12.
7 Frank C. Senn, *The people's work: A social history of the liturgy* (Minneapolis: Fortress Press, 2006), 227.
8 Moore-Keish, *Ritual approach*, 63.

This interpretation of *credenda* LOLC has been challenged by several scholars, including Geoffrey Wainwright[9], Kevin Irwin[10] and Bryan Spinks[11]. For example, Spinks remarks that 'the idea that doctrine only flowed from liturgy and that doctrine never impacted and changed liturgical practice is pious humbug and wishful thinking'[12]. Similarly, Wainwright and Irwin demonstrate that the Latin epigram does not presume liturgical fixity, nor does it mean that the church should draw on liturgical practice as the sole or chief norm for doctrine. Rather, the liturgy expresses the church's faith and may only serve as a source for establishing theology to the degree that it is founded on holy scripture. Wainwright argues that LOLC may be construed in two ways. The more usual way makes the rule of prayer a norm for belief: what is prayed indicates what may and must be believed. But from the grammatical point of view, it is equally possible to reverse subject and predicate and so take the tag as meaning that the rule of faith is the norm for prayer: what must be believed governs what may and should be prayed. The linguistic ambiguity of the Latin tag corresponds to a material interplay which in fact takes place between worship and doctrine in Christian practice: worship influences doctrine and doctrine, worship[13]. Thus, the relationship between theology and liturgy is dialectical: it is a two-way relationship. Wainwright underscores that LOLC is a two-directional principle: theology and liturgy are mutually formative, they are correlative norms.[14]

Another theologian who has weighed in on the issue is Paul Marshall. Marshall delivers a stinging critique of the interpretation of LOLC by Kavanagh and Fagerberg[15]. They present, says Marshall, the liturgy as simply a given that 'the people receive passively, rather than actively participating in the formation and critique of that liturgy'[16].

---

9   Geoffrey Wainwright, *Doxology, the praise of God in worship, doctrine and life: A systematic theology* (New York: Oxford University Press, 1980).
10 Kevin W. Irwin, *Liturgical theology: A primer* (Collegeville: Liturgical Press, 1990).
11 Bryan D. Spinks, *Do this in remembrance of Me: The Eucharist from the early church to the present day* (London: SCM Press, 2013).
12 Spinks, *Eucharist*, 12.
13 Wainwright, *Doxology*, 218.
14 Ibidem, p. 161
15 Moore-Keish, *Ritual approach*, 129-151.
16 Paul V. Marshall, „Reconsidering "Liturgical Theology": Is there a Lex Orandi for all Christians?," *Studia Liturgica* 25 (1995), 134.

To claim that there is 'a one-way street, from the divinely given liturgy to the human response of believing' is to perpetuate 'a view of the liturgy that is fixed, authoritarian, and hierarchical'[17]. Contrary to this interpretation, Marshall claims that Prosper 'never intended to posit liturgical action as the single norm that establishes Christian believing'.[18] Rather, 'Prosper's overall point, arguing against semi-Pelagianism, is that believing is a gift from God, not a human achievement.'[19]

Historical background
The expression LOLC appears to be derived from a fifth century brief work ascribed to Prosper of Aquitaine, a monk in the region of Marseille and secretary to Leo the Great, and fierce adherent to Augustine's theology. That work is known by various titles, including *Indiculus de gratia Dei* and *Epistolae* or *Capitulae Caelestini*. In this writing, Prosper does not mention a LOLC as such but does write *ut legem credendi lex statuat supplicandi*. In chapter eight of his *Indiculus* one finds the following passage:

> Besides the inviolable sanctions of the most blessed and apostolic see, with which the most pious fathers, *having cast down the pride of the pestilential novel teaching, taught us to ascribe to the grace of Christ the origins of good will, the growth of commendable efforts, and perseverance in them to the end,* let us consider the sacraments of priestly prayers that, having been handed down by the apostles, are uniformly practiced throughout the world in every Catholic church, *ut legem credendi lex statuat supplicandi.*[20]

This last expression reads: so that the law [or rule or pattern] of supplicating [not the more general *orandi*, 'praying'] may establish [or confirm] the law [or rule or pattern] of believing [not 'the faith']. Thus, Prosper appeals to the universal liturgical practice of praying for the salvation of all people, 'not because it is the only source, or even the first source, for theological reflection, but because it is a reliable source that demonstrates the broad apostolic Christian faith'[21]. Moreover, he coined it while his controversy with the semi-Pelagians was in the background! Especially

---

17 Moore-Keish, *Ritual approach*, 65
18 Ibidem
19 Ibidem
20 Wainwright, *Doxology*, 225-226.
21 Moore-Keish, *Ritual approach*, 66

when this passage in the *Indiculus* is juxtaposed with a parallel passage in *De vocatione omnium gentium*, one can see that Prosper's referent is very precise. His *lex supplicandi* refers to 1 Timothy 2:1-4. That prayer, those supplications, underscore the Christian belief that grace comes from God through Jesus Christ by the Holy Spirit. Prosper's referent again turns out to be very precise. His *lex supplicandi* refers to Pauls' exhortation in 1 Timothy 2:1-4. This is even more clear when the *Indiculus* is juxtaposed with a parallel passage in *De vocatione omnium gentium*[22]. Prosper's argument is based on Christian prayers of intercession, beseeching God for the conversion of sinners according to the precept of 1 Timothy 2.

Besides this, not all early Christian prayer was liturgical. A direct connection between *lex orandi* and liturgy therefore begs the question. Prosper himself does not give any indication that he was talking about officially sanctioned and corporate prayer within the Roman Mass[23].

Whatever Prosper may have intended by his maxim, however, it has provided the occasion for a modern debate about the relationship between theology (*lex credendi*) and liturgy (*lex orandi*). In which way? Historical research has shown that there was another man, named Dom Guéranger (1805-1875), who was also called Prosper. How ironic history sometimes is! He introduced the much-discussed abbreviated version in his *Institutions liturgiques* - he called it an axiom - and that variant has become popular in discussions about liturgical theology.

So, it is appropriate to give some attention within the context of this volume to the debate about the connection between theology and liturgy that has divided Protestants and Catholics since the time of the Reformation. The Reformers' Catholic opponents usually conceded that, while the substance of their eucharistic theology had its foundation in scripture, there were aspects of the Mass (such as the Roman Canon) that had developed over time. Like their medieval forebears, 16th century Catholic apologists assumed that the *lex orandi* should determine the *lex credendi*. Scripture was a source of Catholic doctrine but so were the liturgical practice of the church and the testimony of the fathers. Thus the fact that many Catholic liturgical practices had no explicit scriptural

---

22 Daniel G. Van Slyke, "Lex orandi lex credendi: Liturgy as Locus Theologicus in the fifth century?," *Josephinum Journal of Theology* 11 (2004), 131.

23 Van Slyke, „Liturgy as Locus"; Paul de Clerck, „Lex orandi, lex credendi: The original sense and historical avatars of an equivocal adage," *Studia Liturgica* 24 (1994), 178–200.

warrant was not necessarily problematic for Catholic apologists[24].

On the other hand, the Reformers believed that certain biblical doctrines were incompatible with various liturgical practices in the Roman church. For example, the Roman Mass—particularly the sacrificial language of the Latin canon—was hardly compatible with the doctrines of the perfection of Christ's atonement and of justification by faith alone. Like the gift of justification, Protestants saw the Lord's Supper as a gift (*beneficium*) received from God and not a sacrifice (*sacrificium*) offered to God. Protestant theology, therefore, inevitably led to changes in liturgy. Hence, the Reformers believed that *lex credendi* could exercise control over *lex orandi* 'when it came to forms of existing worship that needed correction'[25]. Theology can critique worship and improve it wherever and whenever necessary.

The Latin maxim LOLC thus offers a helpful corrective to the common tendency in modern Protestant circles to bifurcate theology and liturgy as two independent branches of ecclesial life. Theology and liturgy are, in fact, interrelated and mutually formative. True doctrine forms the foundation of true worship, and true worship is an expression of true doctrine. Theology shapes the church's liturgy but, over time, the worship of the church will inevitably influence its theology.

Perspective from Hebrews

How on Earth Did Jesus Become a God? This is the provocative title of Larry Hurtado's thought provoking study on the person of Christ[26]. He examines the keen devotion to Jesus that emerged with surprising speed soon after his death. Reverence for Jesus among early Christians, as Hurtado notes, included grand claims about Jesus' significance (*lex credendi*) and a pattern of devotional practices (*lex* ordandi) that effectively treated him as divine. In a previous publication, *One God, One Lord*[27], he already mentions six specific devotional practices related to the person of Jesus Christ as God:

---

24 Nicholas Thompson, *Eucharistic sacrifice and patristic tradition in the theology of Martin Bucer, 1534–1546* (Leiden: Brill, 2005), 4-5.
25 Irwin, *Liturgical theology*, 16.
26 Larry W. Hurtado, *How on earth did Jesus become a God? Historical questions about earliest devotion to Jesus* (Grand Rapids: Eerdmans, 2005).
27 Larry W. Hurtado, *One God, one Lord: Early Christian devotion and ancient Jewish monotheism* (Minneapolis: Fortress Press, 1998).

- Hymns about Jesus as part of early Christian worship;
- Prayer to God 'through' Jesus and 'in Jesus' name', and even direct prayer to Jesus himself, especially the invocation of Jesus in the setting of corporate worship;
- Calling upon Jesus: baptism, healing and exorcism;
- A common Christian meal enacted as sacred where the risen Jesus presides as 'Lord';
- Confessing Jesus in the context of Christian worship;
- Christian prophecy as oracles of the risen Jesus and the Holy Spirit understood as the Spirit of Jesus[28].

This early Christian theology stems from early Christian worship, and could be named a kind of liturgical theology. So, then, Jesus became a God in the lives of so many people, but for what reasons? At this point we turn to the letter to the Hebrews, because this is exactly where Hebrews offers a wonderful answer. Let this sermon – as this letter in itself sounds – inform us of its answer by connecting the exposition in Hebr.1:1-4 with its application in 2:1-4:

> 1 Long ago, at many times and in many ways, God spoke to our fathers by the prophets,
> 2 but in these last days he has spoken to us by his Son, whom he appointed the heir of all things, through whom also he created the world.
> 3 He is the radiance of the glory of God and the exact imprint of his nature, and he upholds the universe by the word of his power. After making purification for sins, he sat down at the right hand of the Majesty on high,
> 4 having become as much superior to angels as the name he has inherited is more excellent than theirs.
> (Hebr. 1:1-4)

First and foremost, there is no *lex credendi* that existed already here, but God 'exists' – He *is* - and *God has spoken* (*ho lalèsas*) or even in the present tense, He is 'The One Who is Speaking' (see 12:25).

> 1 Therefore we must pay much closer attention to what we have heard, lest we drift away from it.
> 2 For since the message declared by angels proved to be reliable, and every transgression or disobedience received a just retribution,

---

28 Hurtado, *Historical questions*, 27-28; Hurtado, *Early Christian devotion*, 100-114.

> 3 how shall we escape if we neglect such a great salvation? It was declared at first by the Lord, and it was attested to us by those who heard,
> 4 while God also bore witness by signs and wonders and various miracles and by gifts of the Holy Spirit distributed according to his will.
> (Hebr. 2:1-4)

The Hebrew congregation started to pray to Jesus, sing their songs, make their confession of faith - due to the fact that God has spoken in the Son. A *lex audiendi*, then, precedes both *lex credendi* and *lex orandi*. However, what is the situation in this congregation according to the text of this sermon?

> 1 Therefore, while the promise of entering his rest still stands, *let us fear lest any of you should seem to have failed to reach it.*
> 2 For good news came to us just as to them, but the message they heard did not benefit them, because they **were not united by faith** with those who **listened**.
> (Hebr. 4:1-2, my emphasis)

The Hebrews were dull of hearing (5:10), unskilled in the word of righteousness (5:13), and had not gained the power of discernment by means of constantly practicing distinguishing good from evil. All this leads to the great danger of falling away (6:12). What happens in the Hebrew congregation according to the transmogrified LOLC-rule? What was their method of prayer at that very moment in history? There was no living practice of the *lex orandi* left, because their faith had diminished. Sound theology did not come from their worship any longer.

Therefore, time and again they must be admonished 'let us draw near' (e.g. 4:16), 'let us hold fast' (e.g. 4:14) and so forth. They did not realise themselves what it meant to come to the church (12:22-24) and they disregarded the worship service, refrained from it and, in this way, there was no education or formation of the Christian life at all. What did this preacher to the Hebrews therefore do? He started right from the beginning: God speaks. In the form of a great song of love and of knowledge of our great High Priest whom we confess, the letter is clearly meant as a correction to the lived out liturgy. That *lex credendi* could inspire and enliven the *lex orandi*, of which the practice had diminished.

All in all, from the perspective of Hebrews the LOLC-rule should be extended as follows:

> *lex audiendi* <-> *lex orandi* <-> *lex credendi* <-> *lex vivendi*.

That is, the rule states: from listening to living via liturgy and love, and the other way round. All parts are interconnected as a four-leaf clover. The heart of this clover is our heavenly High Priest in heaven whose service is 24/7/365.

It is all about the formation of faith, in classrooms as much as in sanctuaries. To hold these four - the *audiendi*, the *orandi*, the *credendi*, the *vivendi* - in a creative tension by means of a critical conversation is the wonderful ongoing task of practical theology.

The Use for Education and Formation

This brief introduction to the current use and the history of the LOLC-rule shows us the real danger of parroting as a threat to the process of formation. The initial words have been changed out of their original context as has been shown. Nevertheless, the abbreviated rule does remind us of the great importance of holding doctrine and faith, principles and practices together. On the basis of the current use of LOCL-rule as seen from both, the perspective of history and the letter to the Hebrews, I offer the following four practical-theological considerations for further reflection on the theme of this book, 'education, formation, and the church'.

1. If we allow the 'rule of praying' to determine the 'rule of belief' one-sidedly, Hebrews can show us that we ultimately can believe everything and so we will believe nothing at all. Hebrews emphasises the great importance of listening to the *verbum externum* as the *viva vox dei*, considering the process of ormation as practical education in church, at schools and at home. The German theologian Bernd Wannenwetsch therefore rightly emphasises the necessity of starting with and thinking from *the verbum externum* and not from 'felt needs', 'religious experiences' or some such. 'From a theological point of view, the choice to take the religious market as a starting point has an even more problematic consequence. By offering the gospel in a market of competing religious players, the church has ceased to consider and receive this gospel as God's own Word'[29]. In sum: listening according to Hebrews is an exercise in practical theology to

---

29 Bernd Wannenwetsch, „Inwardness and commodification: How romantic hermeneutics prepared the way for the culture of managerialism – A theological analysis", *Studies in Christian Ethics* 21 (2008), 37.

revive the living faith, an exposition of truth directed to the correction of that congregational practice suffering *acedia*. This 'word of exhortation' (*parakalein*; 13:22) appears to be an admonition: acting as a warning as well as an encouragement.

2. One could argue that the *lex orandi* is a prerequisite for the *lex credendi*, at least in the sense that, without prayer, we will not understand what we believe at all. A theological discussion is not a substitute for knowing God. If you are a theologian, you pray truly. And if you pray truly, you are a theologian. An active life of prayer before God sits at the centre of a disciple's existence. Prayer is the core spiritual discipline indeed. Prayer pursues and blossoms in knowledge of God through dialogue and listening, silence and speech. Surely, the way of praying does influence what we believe. How many prayers of mothers are a great blessing in the faith formation of their children and youngsters. They hear how we appeal to God, and even in our voices our deepest convictions of love and fear, hope and distress, and so forth, are heard. The teaching ministry of the congregation could not function as a real blessing without these practices. But, how do we address God? Is there not the great danger that we might pray to an idol because we project our ideas on a 'God' who is *not there*? The God 'who is there' has revealed in himself in and by his Word, but human beings always are prone to create God after his or her own image, the image by which they grew up with or just the opposite as reaction to the upbringing. Here the need of the theology of the Spirit comes in. The Spirit works in order to coin time and again the image of God after the image of Christ. Therefore, the *lex credendi* is definitely important for the well-being of the *lex orandi*.

3. We saw something of the formative effect of liturgy, which is related to the relationship between liturgy and theology. Pleadings are made e.g. by the Liquid Church Movement[30] to make church services less 'high ecclesiastical', formal and impersonal. Accessibility, spontaneity and a more informal gathering would benefit the personal experience of faith. Such a plea affects the order of service, but also the use of language and the choice of music. A more familiar gathering calls for a less 'hallowed space'. Church buildings are too distant. The theological foundation then rests on the *anthropogenesis* (incarnation) of Jesus Christ. Just as He became human among people and approached people in their everyday lives, so should

---

30 Pete Ward, *Liquid Church* (Eugene: Wipf and Stock Publishers, 2002).

we as churches. The church, in His footsteps, should adapt to today's culture and everyday life. More informal gatherings are also more attractive to outsiders. Moreover, the congregation is referred to as the 'household of God'. If God is our Father and we are His children, then the right atmosphere is more one of intimacy, warmth, and casualness. While, according to these voices, current liturgical customs encourage alienation.

The danger of unnecessary formalism and ritualism is indeed present in congregational meetings. Our salvation does not lie in forms and customs. But an appeal to the Incarnation of Christ as done by the Liquid Church Movement misses the ascension of our King. Jesus' ascension connects the earthly liturgy with the heavenly liturgy, as is shown in and is the basis of the letter to the Hebrews (especially 8:1; 12: 22-24). And that is why respect, dignity and the awareness of proper distance are essential to our worship. The celestial liturgy could not be called every day or informal. There is still reason to be deeply impressed by who God is. This requires respect and awe (12:29-29). This awareness has a shaping effect and also calls for reformation in places where these notions have disappeared. For a vision of liturgy we cannot stop at the coming of Jesus to earth, but must do justice to Jesus' heavenly place.

This also applies to for example a one-sided image of a Father-child relationship. An appeal to God as Father should at least go hand in hand with the answer to the question: 'Am I then a Father, where is My honour? And am I a Lord, where is My fear?' (Malachi 1:6). To call upon God as Father means: '... so walk in fear into the time of your indwelling' (1 Peter 1:17). Thus Peter concludes that to a holy God belongs a holy people. This is by no means a commonplace. After all, a 'holy people' is just a 'people apart'. i.d. they are set apart by God to live for Him.

Therefore, all God's virtues (qualities, characteristics) should determine the character of our meetings in a tension of proximity and distance. Certainly, the Holy One has come to man, but that does not erase the distance between God and men. There undoubtedly is an intimate relationship e.g. between Abraham and the LORD. The LORD speaks with Abraham as with a friend. Yet Abraham says: 'I have hurt myself to approach unto thee, though I am dust and ashes' (Genesis 18:27). A close relationship with God does not mean that there are two friends on an equal footing. There is also a side of the ecclesiastical spectrum where God seems to be exclusively 'at a distance'. Very lofty and holy, sovereign and severe, almost incalculable because of hidden decisions. A church service then almost gets something icy. That can become the surrogate for reverence. In such a case there is also an urgent need for an adjustment of the image of God.

Our God is very exalted and very near. For a healthy biblical theology of congregational meetings, the wording in Isaiah 57:15 is of great significance: 'For thus says the One who is high and lifted up, who inhabits eternity, and whose name is Holy: I dwell in the high and in holy place, and also with him who is of a contrite and lowly spirit, to revive the spirit of the lowly and to revive the heart of the contrite.'

4. From the proposed mutual reciprocal relation between the *orandi* and the *credendi* in the life of the church as a whole, I turn for a moment to our theological training institutes, theological departments of a university or whatever. Just three remarks, which may be seen as a bucket list for the field of homiletics and liturgy:

a) In our theological education the interrelatedness of *meditatio* and *disputatio* is paramount. The Middle Ages reflects a separation between them, due to the fact that *meditation* seems to be at home in cloisters (as the 'lex orandi') and *disputations* in universities (as the 'lex credendi'). This division still has great consequences, even in the field of practical (!) theology. For instance, too often, using so-called scientific (exegetical) methods and personal meditation are separated in the homiletical processes of preparation of the sermons. The suggestion behind this divide is the distinction between 'objective' and 'subjective' truth, which distinction and ultimately the division has been introduced by René Descartes in the 17th century and has influenced so much scientific and ecclesial practices[31]. The understanding of the LOLC rule as seen in this chapter will be able to bridge the gap between these distinctions that are profoundly inseparable and mutually effect each other. The 'objective' theological truth is a 'subjective' believed and experienced truth in faith practices, e.g. praying and singing, and the other way round, the 'subjective' experienced and believed truth has led to and still leads to the 'objectives' of faith as expressed in theology.

b) Singing and saying, therefore, are both necessary for a sound theology. '*Theologein*' ultimately is *doxologein* or it is nothing at all, for to practise theology is to speak of God who is beyond our comprehension. In Hebrews, sayings about Jesus Christ function as songs. In the Early Church, *theologein* and *hymnein* are intertwined. Accordingly, theology 'as a concept in Christianity was first understood in the sense of a hymnal "calling God", in which the pronouncing of God's name

---

31 Charles Taylor, *A secular age* (Harvard: Harvard University Press, 2007).

aimed at the presence of God himself and did not make him for instance the "object" of a *logos, about* which one thinks or speaks'[32].

c. The importance of combining liturgical 'poetry' and theological/ doctrinal 'prose'. Worship is the main vehicle of Christian theology, because there are quite a few people who do not read any theological books on a regular basis. In our worship, there should be room for imagination to stir up the life indicated by *lex orandi* as well as the teaching ministry marked by *lex credendi*. To create room for a life of listening there should be, in our services, more room for silence, for preparing hearts and moving our thoughts.

All in all, the LOCL-rule is a thought provoking rule and does inform and form our believes and practices in classrooms and congregational meetings. Even our personal devotions are formed by the '*lex credendi, lex orandi*' in a life which is exposed to the *lex audiendi* and explained by the *lex vivendi* as seen from the perspective of Hebrews.

---

[32] Bernd Wannenwetsch, „Singen und Sagen. Zur musisch-musikalischen Dimension der Theologie," *Neue Zeitschrift für Systematische Theologie und Religionsphilosophie* 46 (2004), 335.

7. Formation Activities Considered through the Lenses of Attitudes, Cognition and Perception – Elucidation from the Perspective of the Letter to the Hebrews

Ferdi Kruger

Introduction: Problem Statement and Central Theoretical Argument
In scrutinizing aspects such as education formation, and the Church, one could easily overlook obvious factors like attitudes, cognition, and perceptions. In fact, each topic could justify a paper on its own. This article addresses the interrelated coherence of these factors. It is written from a practical theological viewpoint, with a particular interest in whether the idea of transformative education could resonate with these three determining aspects in daily life. Transformation is, after all, part of life, and a reconceptualization of the discipline of practical theology is necessary to identify pointers that are influenced by people's attitudes for a meaningful contribution to the discourse on transformative education.[1] It was Phyllis Tickle,[2] amongst others, who convincingly identified the so-called 500-year cycles of transformation in the history of Christianity, which underline the importance of the Christian faith continuing to be translated and continuously entering into and interacting with the vernacular culture else it withers and fades. The emphasis on engaging with culture and societal challenges is simultaneously challenging for theological education because it seems like education does not solely prepare students for professional careers or ministry. The current exchange of views on the idea of transformative education includes

---

[1] Jurgens Hendriks, "Practical theology '[re]entering vernacular culture?' New frontiers and challenges to doing theology as life goes on," HTS Teologiese Studies/Theological Studies (2017), 1.
[2] Phyllis Tickle, The great emergence: How Christianity is changing and why (Baker, Grand Rapids, 2008).

emphasis that education deeply affects a change in the perspective and frame-reference of students.

An increasing emphasis on current trends is challenging for the praxis of students, who should become actively engaged in new avenues for transformation.[3] Dames,[4] for example, explicated that practical theology is about life and death. This very fact urges practical theologians to reflect on whether this discipline has indeed contributed to spiritual, socio-economic, political, moral, and cultural realities in society. Renewed interest in transformative education, an emerging technological revolution[5] called the Fourth Industrial Revolution, is currently being discussed. It comes down to a blurring of lines between the physical and digital spheres. It is clear that technology in the digital environment has influenced people's lives more deeply than the naked eye can see. The emphasis on technology and innovation is aimed at improving people's quality of life. Still, it has profound consequences for the way people learn and how they interact.[6] While scholars are still reflecting on the possible impact of the Fourth Industrial Revolution and whether it has transformed quality of life for humans or students, scholars have already started to debate the idea of a Fifth Industrial Revolution, namely the era of artificial intelligence. In the Fifth Industrial Revolution, humans and machines have danced more closely together, metaphorically speaking. On a critical note, while the role of humans could be seemingly underplayed within the Fourth Industrial Revolution, the aim of the Fifth Industrial Revolution has already highlighted an increased awareness of human responsibility.

Hence, transformative education within this particular context of rapid changes inevitably considers the notion of formation, which has to do with students' thoughts, feelings, and actions in the midst of what they are experiencing daily. Therefore, transformative education aims to alter people's ways of being in this world. It further enhances the opportunity to cultivate a new mindset and understanding of what is happening. The previous paragraphs have indicated the reality of the rapid changes students are exposed to in their lives. Consequently, one has to acknow-

---

3 Elizabeth Mackinlay and Katelyn Barney, "Unknown and Unknowing Possibilities: Transformative Learning, Social Justice, and Decolonising Pedagogy," Indigenous Australian Studies, Journal of Transformative Education 12 (2014), 54–73.
4 Gordon Dames, "'Quo Vadis' Practical Theology?: A response," Scriptura 100 (2009), 81–88.
5 Cf. Brende and Borge, *Global Risks Report*, 22.
6 Phil Mjwara, "White Paper on Science, Technology and Innovation," 11.

ledge that changes in society are simultaneously challenging for education.[7] Theological education aimed at training ministers is constantly searching for a new model for ministers' training. The concern for this particular context of successive revolutions, influencing theological education should lead to a commitment to rethinking the outcome of ministers' education. It is a fact that whether in a crisis or merely a painful transition, many churches, Christian groupings, and theological institutions are reconsidering their theological education and ministerial formation programmes to adequately address the challenges offered by societal changes.[8] Additionally, many schools of theology are re-envisioning theological education as a formational activity, an activity based on the assumption that the students' appropriation of theology is the most central aspect of theological training.[9] Theological education then becomes an instrument of a broad-based formation process that ensures that ministerial candidates are adequately formed to serve as vanguards for the transmission and survival of a particular Christian tradition.[10]

Cognisance of the trends mentioned above offers the opportunity to mention the research question identified for this research. The problem statement for this research is as follows:

What kind of insight could the concepts of attitude, cognition, and perception, as reflected in the Letter to the Hebrews, offer on the importance of formation activities?

In addressing this problem, insight into the piercing perspectives provided by the Letter to the Hebrews on how an understanding of formation activities, dealing with the concepts underlined in the research question, could further enhance an integrated view of the contours of practical theological education. The purpose of the Letter to the Hebrews has been understood as seeing that the message of Christ, even within the culmination of troublesome circumstances and demanding challenges,

---

7   Cf. Dames, "'Quo Vadis' Practical Theology? A response," 87.
8   Marilyn Naidoo, "Persistent issues impacting on the training of ministers in the South African context," Scriptura 112 (2013), 1.
9   Paul Watson, "Making Christians: An Interview with John Westerhoff," Leaven 4, no. 3 (2012). http://digitalcommons.pepperdine.edu/leaven/vol4/iss3/6
10 Naidoo, "Persistent issues impacting on the training of ministers in the South African context," 2.

has meaningful relevance for the listeners of the letter.[11] What follows now will be organised according to a qualitative literature study; in this process, the exploration of knowledge in the field will be acknowledged.[12] The latter will be organised and critically interpreted in light of the research problem.

Conceptual Framework: Views of Piaget and Vygotsky on Cognition and Perceptions that Unlock the Operation of Schemes and Inner Speech
The renewed interest in transformative education that we need to realise is closely linked to Mezirow, a sociologist who studied adults in the environment of continuing education.[13] Transformative learning allows students to use the contexts of their formal learning experiences to construct and reconstruct personal meaning.[14] Mezirow's view is based on ideas that were originally developed by Habermas, who was interested in communicative competence. Mezirow elaborated on this idea and defined both the domains of learning and reflective discourse as core concepts of adult learning within a transformative learning theory.[15] Meaningful learning, after all, goes beyond mere knowledge acquisition to qualify for a career. This kind of learning entails making interpretations from the student's own beliefs and judgments and consciously defining the meaning of their own experiences[16] as well as the meaning of their own lives.[17-18] Transformative education wants students to challenge

---

11 Donald Guthrie, Hebrews, in Tyndale New Testament Commentaries (Grand Rapids: Eerdmans, 1996), 117
12 Cf. Y. Bothma, M. Greeff, F.M. Mulaudzi, and S.C.D Wright, Research in Health Sciences, Cape Town: Pearson.
13 Mezirow, J. Fostering critical reflection in adulthood: A guide to transformative and emancipatory learning (San Francisco, CA: Jossey-Bass, 1990).
14 Chad Hoggan, "Bringing clarity to transformative learning research," Adult Education Research Conference. http://newprairiepress.org/aerc/2015/papers/26.
15 Mezirow, "Fostering critical reflection in adulthood: A guide to transformative and emancipatory learning."
16 M.M. Rahman and A.K.M. Hoque, "Transformative Learning: a concept and powerful vision for adult education," AKMMC J 8 (2017), 128–131.
17 Michael Christie et al., "Putting transformative learning theory into practice," Australian Journal of Adult Learning 55 (2015), 12.
18 Will McWhinney and Laura Markos, "Transformative Education: Across the Threshold," Journal of transformative education, 1 (2003), 17.

certain assumptions and, where applicable, change them to enhance their quality of life.[19]

Moreover, Mezirow's theory argues that every individual has a particular view or perception of the world. The particular worldview may or may not be well articulated. Still, it is usually based on a set of paradigmatic assumptions derived from the individual's upbringing, life experience, culture, or education.[20] If the individual is especially committed to a worldview, a proselytising element will likely creep in. Mezirow claimed that individuals have difficulty changing because their worldviews become unconscious frames of reference. An essential component of Mezirow's theory is the need to develop communicative skills so that internal and external conflicts, which result from changes in perspective, can be resolved via rational discourse rather than by utilizing force. However, people are involved in communities of practice everywhere and are generally engaged in some of them, whether at work, school, home, or in civic life.[21] For a community of practice to function, it needs to generate and appropriate a shared repertoire of ideas, commitments, and memories. It also needs to develop various resources, such as routines, vocabulary, and symbols, that contain the community's accumulated knowledge. In other words, it involves practices, or ways of doing and approaching things that are shared to some significant extent among members.[22] [23] Mezirow argued that every individual has a particular view (attitude or perception) of the world that is derived from their upbringing, education, or concrete life experiences.[24]

People's attitudes, cognition, and perceptions are influential in the formation of students in education. The formation is, after all, a life-long process, and within the education environment, lecturers and students build the learning experience on previous attitudes, cognitions, and perceptions. A simple definition of an attitude is a mindset or a tendency to act in a particular way due to an individual's experience and temperament.[25] Attitudes are a complex combination of things we call

---

19 Michael Christie et al., "Putting transformative learning theory into practice," 12.
20 Michael Christie et al., "Putting transformative learning theory into practice," 11.
21 M.K. Smith, "Communities of practice," The encyclopaedia of informal education (2003). www.infed.org/biblio/communities of practice.htm.
22 M.K. Smith, "Communities of practice."
23 J. Lave and E. Wenger, Situated learning. Legitimate peripheral participation (Cambridge: University Press, 1991).
24 Mezirow, *Fostering*, 23
25 Andrew Pickens, Attitudes and perceptions (Deutsches Institut for fur Wirtschaftsforschung, 2015), 44.

personality, beliefs, values, behaviours, and motivations. An attitude includes three components: an effect (a feeling), a cognition (a thought or belief), and behaviour (an action).[26] Changes in one of the components will inevitably influence the other components. Cognition constitutes the process through which people think about and make sense of other people, themselves, and their social situations. Cognition is essential to one's knowledge of human beings and life because it is the mental representation through which people make contact with the world. The vital thing to note is that cognition should not merely be regarded as an intellectual (cognitive) concept.[27] Rather, the mind, heart, and willingness to act should be seen as vital components of cognition.

Perception can also be described as the eye or the lens to how attitudes and cognition function. Perception is a manner of interpreting sensory information.[28] However, perception is also closely related to people's attitudes. Perception is the process through which people interpret and organise sensations to produce a meaningful world experience.[29] The functioning of the three concepts of attitudes, cognition and perceptions could be distinguished from each other but it is impossible to separate the three concepts. The three concepts work in a tripartite interrelationship. It is essential to realise that the concepts of formation and theological learning are often described differently. Sometimes, theological education is seen as a process that results in learning, and at other times, it is defined as the goal of learning. It is essential to realise that formation should be defined as either intended or unintended, as it is the process through which a person develops a relationship with reality through acquired knowledge, behaviour, and practices.[30] My personal view on the relationship between teaching, learning, and formation is that teaching and learning are integral parts of a more significant formation process that starts in childhood.

---

26 Susan Fiske, Social beings. A core motives approach to Social Psychology (Princeton: Wiley & Sons, 2004) 236.
27 M.W. Eysenck and M.T. Keane, Cognitive Psychology (New York: Psychology Press, 2010), 571.
28 Anita Woolfolk, Educational Psychology, (Boston: Pearson, 2007), 251.
29 Dap Louw and David Edwards, Sielkunde. 'n Inleiding vir student in Suider Afrika (Johannesburg: Heinemann, 1998), 711.
30 Jos de Kock and Ronelle Sonneneberg, "Ritual links worship and learning: An empirical and theoretical contribution from the perspective of young people participating in the Lord's Supper," Studia Liturgica, 46 (2016), 71.

The following section offers a brief overview of the views on cognitive development proposed by two pioneers, Piaget and Vygotsky. Although this article aims to provide perspectives from Hebrews, it is helpful to reflect on the ideas of a few influential psychologists because they clarify the importance of context and continuous reflection in best practices within the education environment. Within this section it will be emphasized that the notion of cognitive aspects identified by Piaget was supplemented by Vygotski's idea that cognitive growth is a social mediated activity.

Piagetian Perspectives on Cognitive Development
Piaget argued that people's thinking processes change slowly from birth to maturity because they are constantly trying to make sense of the world.[31] The social transmission of learning from other people is essential because people have to reinvent their interaction with the world when it is missing. People (also students) are born with a tendency to organise their thinking processes into psychological structures, which Piaget called schemas.[32] Schemas are the basic building blocks of thinking, functioning as templates that are useful for people to organise their experiences.[33] Piaget's theory suggests that, through cognitive schemas, we either assimilate new knowledge within existing knowledge due to logical connections or change our cognitive schemas to accommodate new knowledge that does not fit in with students' pre-existing mental schemas. Experience is cumulative, and a child's experiential repository increases as the child progresses through the cognitive stages. As children develop, they learn how to assimilate or accommodate new knowledge.

In this process, people (students) are striving to understand, during which they attempt to fit new information into what they already know.[34] People have to respond to new situations, but they often need a change in existing schemas to do this. Education and formation must consider people's current situation. Therefore, people utilise their existing schemas when they adapt to complex environments. In this sense of the word, schemas could be regarded as previous learning experiences. Furthermore, there is the possibility of cognitive distortions based on prior wrong and distorted schemas as the frame of reference.

---

31 Anita Woolfolk, Educational Psychology, 27.
32 Susan Fiske, "Social beings. A core motives approach to Social Psychology," 233.
33 Dap Louw and Anet Louw, Die ontiwkkeling van die kind en die adolossent (Bloemfonten: ABC printers, 2007), 24.
34 Anita Woolfolk, Educational Psychology, 29.

Thus, learning, viewed from a Piagetian perspective, should comprise students needing to get a sense of what they are experiencing. The need for equilibrium is the driving force in a student's cognitive development. Therefore, cognitive conflicts could be regarded as beneficial because they challenges students to modify their cognitive schemes. The Piagetian view also underlines the idea that lecturers should understand the concept of students actively participating in what is taught to them.

Vygotsky's View on Students' Interactions with other People and their Inner Speech
Vygotsky's theory builds on Piaget's idea of the student (child) as an active learner, but he elaborated on the importance of social interaction within the teaching and learning environment.[35] Vygotsky suggested that new information is linked to prior knowledge. He expanded this to indicate that the learner constructs knowledge based on personal experiences and hypotheses of the environment, testing hypotheses through social negotiation. Vygotsky further referred to children's affinities for private speech, which is vital for their ability to plan and solve problems, something he described as self-regulation.[36] The little voice inside a person's head, or inner speech, is a common everyday experience. It plays a central role in human consciousness in the interplay of language and thought. As such, it can contribute to our understanding of speech representations. It seems that although inner speech is not the basis of thought, it supports many cognitive activities, including memorisation.[37]

Inner speech, also referred to as *verbal thinking, inner speaking, covert self-talk, internal monologue,* and *internal dialogue,* provides people with the ability to identify their thoughts with language and plays an important role in people's functioning.[38] People carry on an intriguing process of inner dialogue during every waking moment. Inner speech seems to be an important part of our daily lives and also for learning experiences because of people's intrinsic tendency to make sense of what is happening. Even though most inner dialogues stay well hidden, inner speech is far

---

35 Irina Verenikina, Vygotsky in twenty first century research (Australia: Wollongong University, 2010), 4.
36 J.F. Ehrichsen, "Vygotskian inner speech and the reading process," Australian Journal of Educational and Developmental Psychology 6 (2006), 12–25.
37 J.F. Ehrichsen, "Vygotskian inner speech and the reading process."
38 A. Roskies, Thought, language and inner speech (Hanover: Dartmouth College Press, 2015).

more critical than most people realise. From early childhood onwards, inner speech plays a vital role in regulating how people think and behave.[39]

Vygotsky further indicated that inner speech is not the mere interior aspect of external speech, but rather a function. Inner speech is, to a large extent, thinking within the atmosphere of pure meanings. For instance, a single word is so saturated with meaning that many words are required to explain it in external speech.[40] This is a continuous movement back and forth from thought to word and from word to thought. Vygotsky, therefore, highlighted the importance of adults and peers in the development of younger people. The idea of assisted learning or guided participation in giving information, prompts, reminders, and encouragement and allowing students to do more on their own comes to the fore in this framework.

It can be concluded that cognition is described as the mental process of acquiring knowledge and understanding through thoughts, experiences, and the senses. On the other hand, perception is the way people judge others with whom they are in contact. A person's attitude to an idea or object determines what the person thinks and feels and how the person would like to behave towards that idea or object.[41] The way students perceive a particular subject determines their success or failure in that subject. Our knowledge influences the way we perceive the world. Thus, perception, attitude, and cognition are closely related to each other. The particular learning strategy adopted by students in a given situation is determined by a complex interaction between the student's pre-existing beliefs about knowledge and learning and the student's perceptions of the learning approach that is required by the educational context.[42] Listening to formation activities can thereby be regarded as one of the perceptual processes of human beings.[43] People (students) utilise their senses to perceive and try to make sense of what they are observing. A person's perception could, however, not be regarded as a faithful version of the facts due to the fact that only the sense of observing is being utilized. The perception could become distorted.

---

39 J.M. Murphy, "Listening in a second language: hermeneutics and inner speech," Canada Journal 6 (1989), 23–38.
40 M.W. Eysenck and M.T. Keane, Cognitive Psychology (New York: Psychology Press, 2010).
41 Wayne Weiten, Psychology (California: Brooks, 1992), 56.
42 Campbell et al., Students' perceptions of teaching and learning: The influence of students' approaches to learning and teachers' approaches to teaching.
43 S. Steinberg, An introduction to communication studies (Kaapstad: Juta, 2011) 69.

The Importance of (Practical) Theology as Illustrated by the Formational Purpose of Preaching from the Letter to the Hebrews

The Letter to the Hebrews seems to be a sermon addressing people in a problematic praxis of decay.[44] The homily is therefore directed toward daily life. The purpose of the author (preacher) is to build the faith community (church) up (formation) with what is being communicated. The preacher could not overlook the difficulties the people are experiencing and should be appropriately functional in the formation process. The urgency in the author's approach is evident from the formulation "see to it, brothers that none of you turn away from God" (Hebrews 2:1). The role and the importance of caring for one another in a situation of decay and doubt are also emphasised in the formulation "encourage one another daily, as long it is called today" (Hebrews 3:12–13). Within the centre of the formation activities in the sermon to the Hebrews lies the notion of care and encouragement. The attitude of the preacher is therefore highlighted, putting the Word perpendicular above people's lives for them to recognize that God is speaking in and through His Son, Jesus Christ (Hebrews 1–3).

The Essence of Cognition within the Framework of Formation in the Letter to the Hebrews

A significant concept of formation is used in Hebrews. Hebrews 3:1-6 uses the verb κατασκευαζω for edification, indicating a particular focus on formation in Hebrews, denoting the idea of preparation. The same concept is also used in the rest of the Bible; for instance, John the Baptist's preparatory work with a view of Jesus' coming to the world. In Hebrews 3, Jesus is described as the One who is building (forming) his house. Closely linked to the idea of preparation is the idea of the equipment of His house. Therefore, the building (formation) of the faith community in Hebrews has a dual meaning of preparation and equipping.[45] Formation, according to the perspective of Hebrews, aims to prepare people for challenges.

It is striking that house and formation are being utilized simultaneously in this letter. The author does not address the listeners from a height, but calls them *holy brothers*. The attitude of speaking to someone as one of

---

44 Andrie du Toit, Hebreërs vir vandag (Vereeniging: CUM boeke, 2002), 19.
45 Ferdi Kruger and Cassie Venter, Die prediking van geloofsverantwoordelikheid: homiletiese perspektiewe vanuit Hebreërs, Praktiese Teologie in Suid-Afrika 21 (2006), p. 55.

them (the house idea) and not addressing them as strangers or aliens is vital to realize.[46] Formation activities will fall short of their most profound purpose if the relational aspect is not honoured. In fact, in Hebrews, it is made clear that God speaks in the last days in and through His Son. Based on this relational aspect, it could be stated that formation activities will not be functional if they are only directed as a clinical aspect (as something that is committed). According to Hebrews, the bond between teacher and learner has a deeper foundation for a special relationship. God's purpose and His destination for His children are standing on the fore, namely set apart for God. Within the author's understanding (cognition) of the listeners, they have a further identity: people who share in the heavenly calling. The use of the word μετοχοι is notable, as it could even denote the idea of being a partner or companion.[47]

Within the author's cognition, the people who are addressed are companions of the King, Jesus Christ. The theme of calling is evident, and the merciful exchange is furthermore striking. In Hebrews 2:14, it is mentioned that Christ has shared in our humanity. Now, it is said that His followers have become His companions in this world.[48] The challenge in this formation process employing this sermon is for listeners to understand (cognition) the unique identity of Christ and their own identity in realising their relationship with Him. The mention of the idea of God's house as an anchor in this context in Hebrews cannot not be ignored. Within God's house, Jesus Christ is the builder, and Moses is only a servant-therapist (θεραπων). This concept of being a servant concerns someone's humble attitude regarding service and could even denote assistance to someone or faithfully conducting one's duties.[49] The one acting as a servant should have this kind of attitude in which healing is becoming essential.[50] To be part of formation activities primarily concerns the recognition of one's attitudes. Therefore, the attitude of being a servant impacts life as such and in transformation. Thus, to be part of formation activities entails enabling people to function within God's house.

---

46 Andrie du Toit, *Hebreërs vir vandag* (Vereeniging: CUM boeke, 2002), 66.
47 Paul Ellingworth, *Commentary on Hebrews* (Michigan: Eerdmans, 1993), 169.
48 Andrie du Toit, *Hebreërs vir vandag*, 67.
49 F.P. Kruger, "Attitude change through understanding (cognition) of the influence of the persuasive language of liturgy," *HTS* 72 (2016), 1.
50 J.P. Louw and E.A. Nida, Greek English lexicon of the New Testament (I) (New York: United Bible Studies, 1989).

Within the purposefulness of a formation activity, the intimate connection between one's understanding (cognition) of being the House of God and one's attitude is highlighted in Hebrews 3:6. Because of the connectedness of being the house, boldness to speak and to help are evident. The assurance of connectedness describe above is the deeper foundation for the boldness to speak. The attitude of παρρησια (courage, boldness) is also highlighted. Courage is one of the key themes within Hebrews. Within this context, it is the opposite of shyness. Among the Greeks, it was regarded as the most significant gift in life. For the Greeks and Romans, speech was also an indicator of one's character and place in society.[51] The word παρρησια implies *saying anything*. This kind of courage or boldness has the foundation of a solid legal basis. The Greek citizens have always dared to speak during public meetings. Within the context of Hebrews, it has to do with the boldness to approach God, and it offers the foundation for supporting each other in courage. The indicative nature of formation is therefore laid, namely boldness in God.

Perspectives from the Letter the Hebrews on How Distorted Perceptions can be Detrimental to Someone's Attitude and Cognition
The Letter to the Hebrews is written or preached to people who have become disheartened due to concrete circumstances. Uncertainty regarding their understanding of difficult circumstances has prompted them to question whether it is still worth being a Christian in the contemporary world.[52] The phenomenological issue of being in the world, but not from the world, has become an intriguing issue. This sermon's listeners miss the good old days. This idea correlates with the insights of Piaget and Vygotsky regarding their views on schemas and the functioning of people's inner speech. The listeners of this sermon steadily and mentally (cognition) tend to begin to decline. They lose their sense of vitality, enthusiasm, and hopelessness as part and parcel of their new frame of reference. They begin to reflect on the magnitude of things. One of the core problematic aspects in their cognition is their perception. In an old dispensation, God's presence was visible through the formation activities and sacrifices performed in the temple. Rituals and symbols have offered a framework in their understanding. Overall, the new dispensation in

---

51 J.F. Hultin, The ethics of obscene speech in early Christianity and its environment (Brill: Leiden, 2008).
52 Simon Kistemaker, Hebrews (Michigan: Baker House, 1984), 5.

Christ and the complex challenges in society have caused big questions regarding meaningfulness.[53]

The mode of formation delivery within Hebrews is preaching. Four words for preaching are utilized within the Hebrews sermon: admonition, talking, proclaiming the Gospel, and witnessing. These words indicate the multifaceted aspects of preaching as a vital activity within the formation activity of upbuilding the community of faith. It is clear from the concept being utilised that formation activities should be straightforward and easy to comprehend. The formation activities within Hebrews concern offering God's Word to people, and the ultimate purpose is the appropriation of the content being offered. All the words for preaching have a close relationship with either the preacher's attitude or the listeners' attitudes.[54] Formation activities take time, and therefore, one's attitude is of paramount importance. The formation activity within Hebrews is formation through preaching (a sermon). Within the formation or shaping of a faith community using a sermon, Christ's function as a priest or liturgist (Hebrews 8) stands central. The choice of the sermon being utilised in Hebrews concerns the persuasion of people to understand (cognition) within their own and unique situation. In this sense of the word, Hebrews contains a sermon (formation) on faith responsibility.[55] The idea of attitude is mentioned seven times within Hebrews and, each time, within the admonishing (parenetic) sections of this book (Hebrews 3:6, 4:11, 4:16, 6:11, 10:19, 10:35 and 13:6). Three words are utilised to highlight the importance of attitudes, namely παρρησια (boldness), θαρουντθας (boldness), and σπουδαζω (diligence to do something).

Van Houwelingen[56] also referred to Hebrews as letters written in sermons that should be heard in faraway places. Within this letter, theological significance should be acknowledged. The author allows scripture itself to do the talking. This sermon in written form has much to say about transformation in arduous times. Hebrews could therefore be regarded as a three-dimensional sermon,[57] as illustrated in the following schematic presentation.

---

53 F.F. Bruce, The epistle to the Hebrews (Michigan: Eerdmans, 1990), 5.
54 C.R. Hume, Reading through Hebrews (London: SCM Press, 1997), 12.
55 Ferdi Kruger and Cassie Venter, "Die prediking van geloofsverantwoordelikheid: homiletiese perspektiewe vanuit Hebreërs," Praktiese Teologie in Suid-Afrika 21 (2006), 56.
56 Rob van Houwelingen, "Riddles around the Letter of Hebrews," Fides Reformata XVI 2 (2010), 2–6.
57 J.C. Coetzee, Gedagtestruktuur van Hebreërs (Potchefstroom: Fakulteit Teologie, 1986), 5.

Within this schematic representation, it is made clear that the present, past, and future are included within the preacher's view of formation. It is also clear that the functions of attitude, cognition, and perception are underlying aspects of the formation activity in Hebrews. The homiletical manner of addressing these crucial aspects deals with the indicative, imperative, and promise elements that indicate the importance of transformation.

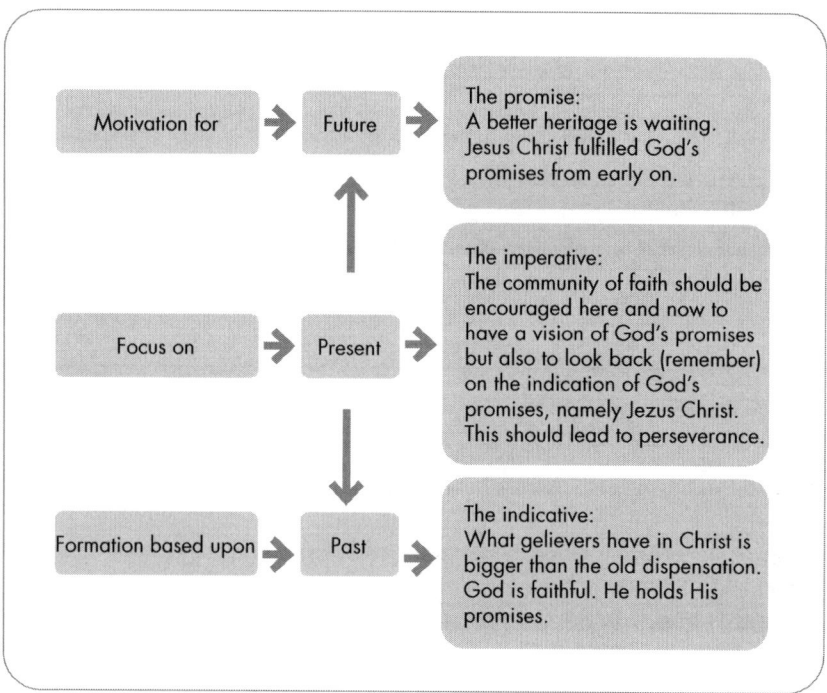

Formation Step by Step and Little by Little—Planning in Action

Hebrews 1:1 offers insight into God's communication in the old dispensation and the new dispensation. It is striking that God has communicated many times and in various ways (*polumeros kai polutropos*; Hebrews 1:1). Within both dispensations, it is God's communication and His Will that should stand central.[58] God never communicated all He had to say at once. The arrow movement in Hebrews 1:1 is visible, namely formation by the prophets, God's formation in and through His Son, formation from the past to the present, and then formation within the

---

58 C.R. Hume, Reading through Hebrews, 14.

living reality of the last days. God communicated in various ways and utilised different modes of formation through learning, comforting, and reprimanding. This sermon to the Hebrews builds on this. The educational principle of starting at the known and moving to the unknown is evident. This principle also influences the preacher in the methodological approach. A creative interrelationship between instruction (doctrinal aspects) and application is apparent (cf. Hebrews 5–10).

Instruction, admonishing, and the purposeful design of the sermon are not everything in the formation process. The concrete context of the listeners enables the preacher to select an appropriate sermon form to connect with the listeners in the midst of what they are experiencing. Various cultural contexts and circumstances necessitate the fact that God has utilised multiple modes of formation. His formation and communication were directed towards people within a particular situation. A definite course of action or planning in God's shaping was evident. God has always worked in a planned and systematic manner.

The Purpose of Formation Activities from Hebrews 5:11-6:2 in Cultivating Discernment
The preacher in Hebrews admonishes the listeners about their laziness or tardiness in listening (νωθρός). The noun laziness (slow to learn) is derived from the field of education.[59] The preacher realised that it is important to adapt to the circumstances of the listeners (audience adaption).[60] Fully aware that depth in the conveyance of this message is not possible, the preacher has to interrupt the process. The author (preacher) has a dual problem; it is crucial to communicate challenging aspects to the listeners in preaching, but the listeners are slow to listen to what the author is offering. The problematic praxis of laziness to listen to the Word of God could not be ignored. Listening to the Word should inevitably lead to obedience to God, and within the context of laziness, a challenge is faced. The listeners to whom the formation activities are delivered have shot themselves in the foot, metaphorically speaking. A relapse in the dynamics of formation activities has to reflect flexibility in one's cognition. At this stage, and on behalf of what the listeners have heard over the years, they should have already been teachers and

---

59 Jerry Vines, The believers guide to Hebrews (New Jersey: Loizeaux, 1993), 89.
60 Jay Adams, Audience adaptions in the sermons and speeches of Paul (Michigan: Baker House, 1976), 13.

lecturers.⁶¹ This tension, however, creates a constant creative challenge to formation activities.

The sermon's listeners have to progress in their growth—growth toward the deeper and fuller content of God's Word. This is typical of spiritual decay; therefore, laziness in listening to God's Word is a *symptom* of spiritual retardation. Learning inertia and thinking laziness were important aspects addressed in this sermon. It is also emphasised that the listeners who are learning from God's Word have learned about theoretical ideas and experienced them in a practical manner (experiential learning). In becoming acquainted with the solid food of the formation activities of preaching, they will eventually distinguish between good and evil in daily life.

A Strategic Revaluation of Formation Activities within Theological Education that Deals with Attitude, Cognition, and Perception

Until now, the research has focused on the importance of the concepts of attitude, cognition, and perception. The importance of the functioning of the mentioned concepts from the viewpoint of social psychology emphasised the idea that education and formation activities could not ignore the fact that the mentioned concepts are influential in the lives of students and lecturers. In section 3, the author indicates that the Letter to the Hebrews is an excellent example of how preaching could shape listeners' lives. Theological training in homiletics and liturgics as branches of practical theology should consider this. The Letter to the Hebrews has offered lecturers the cognisance that formation activities should be realised step-by-step and as planned. Applied to the idea of transformative education, one has to deal with the emphasis on lecturers who should carefully determine which aspects of transformation are evident. To address change, a magnitude of factors related to the attitudes of both lecturers and students and cognition and perception should occur. Transformative education should start with the lecturer, and within the disciplines of homiletics and liturgics, the notion of formation should stand central.

The last part of this paper will be devoted to my view on how these perspectives could enrich practical theological thinking processes. Any discourse in the education process implies an active dialogue with others to better the participatory understanding of the meaning of an experience

---

61 Jerry Vines, The believers guide to Hebrews, 19.

in lecturers' and students' lives.[62] Transformative learning suggests a change in what we know or can do and a dramatic shift in how we come to know and understand ourselves concerning the broader world. Formation activities within the discipline of practical theology are indeed related to communicative acts in the light of the Gospel. According to my understanding, the aspects emanating from this research beneficially reflect this topic. The following sections will apply the elements mentioned above to address how practical theology could contribute to this particular discourse.

Education in Liturgics as Cultivation of Students' Cognition of Daily Life
The information above shows that liturgical formation is not a fixed reality. Having changed and evolved throughout history, just as liturgy itself did, liturgical formation adapts to cultural changes. These changes include, among other things, different ways of transmission and teaching in various cultures, different conceptions of the life of the church, and the different types of addressees: the faithful, the ordained, those in formation, academic teachers, and students. Continuous liturgical formation should involve liturgical activities because by participating in liturgical activities, the mind, emotions, and body of members work together as a holistic entity, as the Body of Christ. Liturgy is continuously formed through interaction, sharing, communion, corporate prayer, familiar stories, and the connectedness of living together.[63]

Continuous formation is what we think or believe and is established by social and physical interaction with the world that we engage through liturgies. The liturgical formation and how people conduct worship services have to reckon with the concepts of attitudes, perception, and cognition. People have to understand what and why they are doing what they are doing to take liturgy to daily life and the streets (liturgy of life and liturgy of the streets). To do this, people (ministers and believers) have to understand how to act. How people are learning within the formation activities of the ministry and the most suitable ways of learning

---

62 Edward W. Taylor and Patricia Cranton (2012), "A content analysis of transformative learning theory," Adult Education Research Conference. http://newprairiepress.org/aerc/2012/papers/47.
63 See B.D. Strawn and W.S Brown, "Liturgical animals: What psychology and neuroscience tell us about formation and worship," Liturgy 28 (2013), 3–14. http://dx.doi.org/10.1080/0458063X.2013.803838.

are also pressing issues. The meaningfulness of the liturgy within changing contexts is a focal point of the teaching and learning environment. Liturgy as a way of life should be facilitated within a learning experience so that an aspect like inter alia transformation within society would not become overwhelming. This could be realised when facilitation of the discipline of liturgics offers perspectives on the continuation of liturgy in daily life for students to become even more aware of the transforming power of liturgy.

Homiletics Optics in Enabling Students with their Cognition, Attitudes, and Perceptions

To preach is to speak in good faith about something that matters to people who attempt to listen/participate in good faith.[64] People listen to recognise God's voice (the Good Shepherd's voice). The attitudes of preachers and listeners, thus, cannot be over-emphasised, as the importance of the preacher's understanding (cognition) of preaching and the perceptions of listeners have to be scrutinised. People, after all, listen to sermons to hear something beyond daily routines and rationalities. Preaching has to make sense for the listeners because it is often a single event or experience in a listener's life that speaks to the sermon's content.[65] When it reflects the Biblical message, religious language opens up a new horizon for people to see a problem in a new light. It can turn things upside down in an unexpected, surprising way.[66] Listeners want to make sense of what is happening in their lives. Wisdom (cognition) for daily life is needed, and from the perspective of the world, it can also be called relevance. How can listeners be helped by sermons about daily life from preachers who are hopeless? What kind of sermon delivery is the most suitable for certain kinds of situations? What kinds of messages are the most suitable in persuading people to change their lives and their attitudes? If preaching intends to change people's lives, the functions and the effects of attitudes, cognition, and perceptions within this process must also be emphasised in the facilitation of the discipline of homiletics.

Homiletical instruction or rationality within this field has traditionally centred on sermon-building (merely cognitive). The student is trained to construct logical outlines and write a logical sermon before delivering the

---

64 A. Deeg, "Viva vox evangelii-reforming preaching," in Preaching God's wisdom, ed. J. Hermelink and A. Deeg (Evangelische Verlaganstalt: Leipzig, 2015), 43–54,
65 A. Deeg, "Viva vox evangelii-reforming preaching," 12.
66 P. Ricoeur, Oneself s another (Chicago: University Press, 1992), 23.

sermon according to sound communicative principles. Such training has commonly produced sermonizers rather than preachers. Students are instructed to prepare sermons that are logical in structure and polished in execution but are utterly harmless when touching the lives of the people. One of the major pitfalls in this kind of education setup is that students are conditioned not to recognize the importance of sermons in enabling listeners to see. In this article, a shift in practical theological reflection has taken place, and a critical emphasis on the public sphere has emerged. In the following sections, visualisation of how the teaching of homiletics could be aligned to be transformative in its effect will be offered. People have to learn to see and describe the world they are living in differently.[67] Practical theological education within the disciplines of homiletics and liturgics could help students realise that the domains represented above could engage in a meaningful manner in helping people in liturgy to look in the right direction. This is actually what happens during, among other things, the act of preaching within the liturgy. God speaks for us to see (to perceive), and opportunities are offered to participants so that they can experience the honour of co-remembering. Memories are part of stories that people tell themselves and each other about the past. People are constantly writing and rewriting the stories of their lives to make sense of the world around them. Thus, their memories become part of this story and their sense-making efforts.[68]

Attitudes, Cognition, and Perceptions within the Formation Activity of Pastoral Care
Pastoral care, as the encounter of the Gospel within people's lives, could be described as a lifelong learning process and an essential aspect within formation activities.[69] In this process, people learn more about God (theological education) and about themselves (anthropology). This happens through the sense of faith. The function of attitudes, the presence of perceptions, and the event of knowing are a few of the fundamental aspects of pastoral care as a discipline. Therefore, Daniël Louw's idea that practical theological reflection should also consider the transformation

---

67 D.J. Smit, Geloof en openbare lewe (Stellenbosch: Sun Press, 2008).
68 G. Rosenwalt and L. Rochberg, Storied Lives (New Haven, CT: Yale University Press, 1992).
69 D.J. Louw, Academic theology: Between sapientia (wisdom) and scientia (science). Theory formation in Practical Theology (University of Stellenbosch: Stellenbosch, 2015).

of human brokenness (the praxis reality of our being human) seems applicable. Our human suffering and the quest for meaning, after all, determine all forms of praxis thinking.[70]

Conclusion
The sections above describe the unique challenge of practical theological education. A mere cognitive approach to exchanging one-sided information should be avoided. The challenge should be to guide students to see the relevance of what is being taught within the concreteness of their lives. It could be summarised in one sentence; namely, practical theological education interested in the formation of students should include the guidance of students to see the impact thereof in their own lives. Within this process, cognisance of the critical functions of attitudes, the power of cognition, and perceptions' colouring is needed. According to the findings of this investigation, the act of formation is dynamic, and above all, the relational commitment of people involved in formation activities is pivotal. The unique relationship between theological faculties and the church was and always will be a critical discourse. Whatever the outcome of this kind of debate, it is clear that theological training has to be purposeful to help students realise the relevance of education for daily life. Transformed attitudes, transformed cognition, and transformed perceptions could open new possibilities.

Keywords: *formation, transformative education, attitudes, cognition, and perceptions, Letter to the Hebrews*

---

70 Daniel Louw, "Habitus in soul care," Acta Theologica 2010, 2.

8. Teaching Social Animals. The role of the school and the church in civic education

Roel Kuiper

Introduction
Many have read *Educated,* the astonishing novel of Tara Westover about a girl who grew up in a Mormon family in Idaho who entered a classroom for the first time when she was already 17 and got her PhD 10 years later, at Cambridge University. She was kept away from school by her parents, who believed that their children would be brainwashed at the public school. Tara's mother offered her a kind of homeschooling, just enough to teach her to read, write and calculate. In fact, all the children in this family were not educated, beginning to work at home at an early age and growing up in isolation, ignorance and in an atmosphere of suspicion of and hostility towards others. When Tara turned 16, however, she decided to go to college and skip high school altogether. She had to take an admission test, not even knowing what a multiple choice test was, and passed. At 17, she walked into the classroom with her contemporaries at Brigham Young University.

What then happened was remarkable and fascinating. There were shortcomings at the level of knowledge, of course. Tara was unaware of the fate of the Jews during World War II and did not know the meaning of the word 'Holocaust'. She could not find her way in the schedules and did not know how to study textbooks. She overcame all of these, though. She passed her first year and proved to be a brilliant student. One of her biggest problems, however, was that she could not adjust to others, even in this Mormon college, where the students shared the same faith. She did not do the 'social' things others did. She was a stranger to others and others were strangers to her. She had no 'repertoire' of practical behavioural concepts that enabled her to participate in social activities.[1] She needed the help of friends to feel safe and to find her way to a doctor or a

---

1 Etienne Wenger, *Communities of Practice. Learning, Meaning, and Identity.* (UK: Cambridge University Press, 1998), 82.

dentist when she needed one. She went through years of therapy before she was able to function normally among others and find her place.

This story offers much for reflection on the social function of education. We are social beings and we learn to live as humans in communities. We are formed, as persons, in interaction with meaningful others, in families and communities. From the early stages of our lives onward, we imitate others' ways and form habits by repeating actions many of which we have picked up or learned from others. While playing with others, we learn to be cooperative; in class, we learn to wait for our turn, realising that a class functions as a group. Social virtues are acquired by example, practice and reflection. John Dewey saw the coordination of individual and social behaviour as central for education. Learning from interaction with others helps us understand others from within by seeing not only their interests but also their thoughts and emotions, and enables us to take all these into account when dealing with others. Ultimately, there is the issue of how to live with others in the wider context of society at large. What does it mean to live with people who are different from us in many ways, with different opinions, but who have the same rights as we do? What does it mean to be a member of society, and what are our responsibilities towards our fellow citizens?

Tara Westover grappled with these issues because she did not go to school earlier in her life. She remained isolated, backward, lonely, with no sense of where to go in life and no purpose because all she had was her family and the limited taste of social life offered by that small circle of relatives. According to Hannah Arendt, *plurality* is a necessary condition to make human action meaningful. It can also be said that others are important for us to confirm who we are and for us to experience being respected for what we are. The reverse is also true: other human beings are important to us because they can receive and complete what we are doing and can give us a sense of being useful, of serving others and of embracing and pursuing a bigger goal in life. We are *social animals,* incomplete by ourselves, in need of others in our emotional, moral, intellectual and socioeconomic life. Christian thinkers call human beings *symbiotics* or *partners* in a common life. But at the same time we know that our capacities for and dispositions towards such have to be trained and formed. According to Gert Biesta, *socialisation* is a task of the school, apart from *subjectification* and *qualification*. Socialisation means finding one's place in society, in the traditions and customs that define who we are and give us a sense of belonging and participation in social practices.

Today, it is held that primary and secondary schools' task of socialisation should include forming pupils' *civic attitudes*. Young people should learn how to behave as citizens, being supportive of society at large and its common values. Behind these desiderata there are serious concerns about the Western society having lost its social cohesion and having become fragmented, falling apart amidst diverging segments and subcultures, leaving people behind and its members not being able to understand or communicate with one another. There are numerous disturbing divisions and examples of public misbehaviour towards others in our late-modern societies, intolerance, hatred and violence in all kinds of break-up relationships, political polarisation and offenses against fundamental human rights, among others. These attitudes, violations and public flaws are seen as a threat to the common good of a peaceful social life. Therefore, schools are requested to form civic attitudes in their pupils and to train them in such so they can align with others in society. In the Netherlands, schools do have the obligation to teach courses on *civic formation* (*burgerschapsvorming*).

In this article, I want to concentrate on the role of Christian schools in *civic formation* as a form of socialisation. I am not addressing the assertion that Christian schools as such contribute to the segmentation of society because they lack the cultural and religious plurality of society at large. I do not think this is the issue because civic attitudes do not start there but from a deeper level of moral and cultural conviction and imagination. Therefore, what I want to examine is the process of moral and cultural formation as part of identity formation in the Christian school. I want to concentrate on the attitudes of solidarity, hospitality and public judgment and ask if and how these can be learned. Then, I want to connect the 'teaching of social animals' with the present interest in Christian practices to serve the common good. The point has been made that Christian education should incorporate these Christian practices and that the Church should be the vanguard of such practices and of the efforts to promote them, but what are the Christian practices that can enable the Church to form civic attitudes in their pupils?

The public function of the school
Before we proceed, we must answer the question of whether the school really has the task of teaching civic attitudes for public life. This question may arise because there is freedom of education and many schools have a private character. Does the world outside bother them? There is a long list of thinkers who have stated that education always ought to be related to

society at large and its interests. Aristotle, to begin with, argued that no citizen should think that he belongs to himself, and considered education a public matter, to be taken care of by the state.[2] Erasmus stated that all children should be educated as if they would serve in the highest offices.[3] We hear of many school reformers in modern times expecting public benefits from a well-organised system of education. Even the anarchist Proudhon presented educational plans to create happiness and solidarity among industrial workers and to improve their conditions.[4] It is undoubtedly true that schools do have a public function: educating children to function well in all kinds of professions in a given society.

In the context of state formation and nation building, governments understand the importance and public power of education. Their interest is to raise citizens who have a sense of belonging to their nation and can contribute to its well-being. Commonality and civil unity are considered important, and so is the creation of civic virtues in the hearts and minds of the new generations. In the Netherlands, those who want to go to the university have to obtain secondary education from schools named *Hogere Burger School* (HBS). This name existed until halfway in the twentieth century. Those schools served civic and social education purposes. Private schools should also contribute to this goal. Among Christians, this was not controversial. The reformed theologian Herman Bavinck, who was interested in education, stated that social education should be valued because we are all members of society and interested in its development.[5] Therefore, he argued that we all need to take a position on all kinds of social issues. Alongside social education, there should even be room for political education. For both, he saw a role for the school and for the Church. The public interests are also the interests of the school and the Church, he claimed.

Bavinck knew that the task of educating the younger generation for their functioning in society must start with reaching out to their souls and hearts, with shaping their character and inner attitudes. We need to foster honest and faithful men and women, he said, people who know what they are obliged to do. Therefore, he claimed that 'justice and love are of more worth for society than knowledge'.[6] According to him, these

---

2 Aristotle, *Politics*, 1337a11.
3 Erasmus, Desiderius, *Tractaat over opvoeding en onderwijs*, par. 64.
4 P.-J. Proudhon, *Selected Writings* (1969), 80–81.
5 Herman Bavinck, *De opvoeding der rijpere jeugd*. (Kok: Kampen, 1932), 187.
6 Ibidem, 188–189.

two are the *social virtues* that all of us specially need. He defined *justice* as giving everyone his or her share, and reminded us to be modest, kind and polite. As for love, he defined it as growing in reverence for, trust in, loyalty to and compassion for others. He added that we are members of several communities and that growing up means growing into these communities. This happens when we practice the aforementioned social virtues and achieve such kind of civility. Education should support this to promote the common good.

Today, many educators and politicians are deeply convinced that the kind of education described above is needed. In classrooms, in the media, on the streets and in business and politics, there are many people who do not behave in a civilised or socially acceptable way. It is also almost taken for granted in today's society that people should primarily serve their own interests. There is a sense that public life is jeopardised by this. In the Netherlands, since 2006 schools have been given the task of fostering *active citizenship*. That is, the school, as an instrument of education, has to respond to social issues. According to official explanations of this, such task has at least three elements: (1) preparedness and ability to become part of the wider community and to contribute to it; (2) social integration of people with different backgrounds and (3) promotion and acceptance of basic values and attitudes belonging to a democratic society.

Schools are free to train their pupils in the way they want to, according to their own standards and values. What and how can the Christian school contribute to public civility, and what is the role of the Church as a public institution? Is it to prepare the pupils well for public conduct and public civility?

Public conduct and moral formation
Public conduct is behaviour towards people who do not belong to our own family or group, people who may be different from us in their opinions, beliefs and habits. We often do not know these people personally, and the only thing we share with them is our public life. That is, we share the same rights and freedoms, we all have to obey the same laws and we are all requested to support common interests. In our public conduct, we not only have to respect others; we also have to accept our role of cooperating and of carrying out the responsibilities that come with this role. Active citizens exercise these rights and pursue their public life in this manner. They reach out and extend all sorts of mutual help in lively neighbourhoods, and pursue social and economic welfare; in short, the common good. The set of roles and behaviours pertaining to this role I

will call a public *repertoire*, following Etienne Wenger. A repertoire gives a clue regarding how to participate and how to respond to expectations, having scripts and concepts for possible conduct and the know-how to engage in the pursuit of the common good.

My point is that being prepared to take the aforementioned role requires a moral attitude. Civic attitude is a species of moral attitude, which is partly a result of identity formation. To become social, one should acquire the know-how to behave in public, and this requires personal formation. The story of Tara Westover shows the need for such formation. She was not ready or prepared for public life and did not know what she had to do in social situations. She had grown up without having seen examples of such, and thus had no *repertoire* for action. Identity formation is about our individual behaviour and our personal values and the way we uphold them. We take our virtues, character, personality and beliefs with us to the public square. These all require the shaping and formation of our *moral capital* in different social situations: family, school, church and society.

Civic attitudes are formed in and through *practices*. Our public conduct is always social and cooperative. We need to work together as partners to fulfil our daily needs and promote the common good. The *repertoire* of public conduct provides scripts that are appropriate in such practices. They focus on things like services for people who need support; clean neighbourhoods; the maintenance of public facilities, schools or healthcare institutions; public justice; environmental issues and others. They reflect the underlying values, interests and goals to be pursued. They entail scripts of behaviour. By this is meant behaviour in the public realm and therefore always in relation to public authorities, within the context of law and constitution. Participation through scripts is enabled by this repertoire.

How can Christian schools prepare their pupils for active participation in public life? It was Nicholas Wolterstorff, among others, who challenged Christian schools to see the needs of the world and educate children for the public benefit. He had a strong idea that motivated him to promote this: the cultural mandate. It is the biblical task of Christians to serve and do justice to others and to all of creation. Christians should respond to situations that are wrong, distorted or oppressive and should actively carry out all kinds of healing and restoring practices, working for the betterment of the world. Christians are 'called to engage in the endeavour and struggle to bring about shalom.'[7] Education following the cultural mandate should prepare for *responsible action*. Undoubtedly, Wolterstorff added something to the debate about *active citizenship*: a sense of calling and direction. Christians are citizens with a calling to fulfil cultural and public duties. He wanted the Christian school to educate for shalom, working for justice and peace.

Wolterstorff, with Bavinck and other Christian thinkers, understood that educating for shalom would require moral formation, the formation of character. 'What sort of person is an ethical person?'[8] How can we cultivate the disposition 'to struggle for the rights of the little ones on earth'? The 'formative strategy' that Wolterstorff proposed is 'tendency learning', strengthening our inclinations to act.[9] This consists of three elements to be applied in education: practical reason, discipline and modelling. For practical reason, pupils should be informed of and convinced about the sort of action that is needed. For discipline, pupils need to be directed and trained to act in certain ways. Lastly, for modelling, pupils need be provided with examples of the conduct and practices they are encouraged to learn. In his early writings, Wolterstorff always mentioned these three *shapers* of our dispositions. Later, when he became somewhat disappointed about the response to his proposals, he added *empathy* and *conversion* to the list of elements to be applied in education for *tendency learning*. By *empathy* as an element of such he meant making pupils experience situations of poverty, humiliation and injustice, and he included *conversion* because he understood that the training of moral character ultimately does not depend on do's and don'ts, not even on models or examples, but on a *converted heart*.

Wolterstorff's belated inclusion of *a converted heart* among the elements of *tendency learning* shows that there was a missing link in the chain in the beginning. Wolterstorff talked about inclinations and certain dispositions, but he had overlooked the person who should be formed. He was focusing on duties and obligations in the world, not on identity formation. His mind was circling around action, assuming that what was required for that action was already included in the person hearing the call of the cultural mandate. Moral attitudes, however, result from deeper

---

7 Nicholas Wolterstorff, *Educating for Shalom. Essays on Christian Higher Education*. (Grand Rapids: Eerdmans, 2004), 143.
8 Ibidem, 137.
9 Nicholas Wolterstorff, *Educating for Responsible Action*. (Grand Rapids: Eerdmans, 1980), 4.

movements of the soul, and with regard to such, much still has to be done. Therefore, Wolterstorff came to see that something like *conversion* was needed. Before dispositions can be cultivated, the person's heart and desires should be touched. These are topics we nowadays have in mind when we talk about identity formation. I want to focus on this matter now. There has been much new insight in this area of late, and I want to add my ideas to what others have said on this matter.

It should be clear that identity formation and socialisation are correlated because we discover what kind of person we are through our participation in communities, in relation and dialogue with others, against social backgrounds, living up to broader human ideals and expectations. Our character and attitudes are formed in the same process, and the identity we take on expresses itself in our social conduct. Identity formation, however, is the most fundamental process. The human person responds *by heart*. It is the heart that decides what kind of person we want to be and how we want to be part of the wider community. The heart, however, can be influenced, animated and filled. This is the work of human formation: shaping someone's identity. What, then, is identity formation?

Identity formation and human flourishing

Simply put, identity formation, of course, is the formation of the human person. Formation is not *making* someone, as if a person is in the power of the educator, a piece of wax, someone to be modelled. Formation happens in a process of interaction, in relationships and with respect to the person to be formed. We confess that every person is created by God in his or her own way, with talents and capacities that are unique, called to respond in a loving way to others and the world. Christian education aims to form a person into one who is aware of this call and is able to respond to it in appropriate ways. Identity formation starts with the notion that human beings are free and responsible. There must be respect and room for spiritual, moral and cultural self-reflection to understand one's motives, choices and reactions. The proper conditions for a person to grow in ways that fits him or her must be set. However, formation is a cooperative process; we are formed by and through others. Others offer us their loving care, examples, goals, narratives, resources and ideas that are important for us to confront. Formation means growing from what we have to stomach and being rubbed and polished to get things right with us.

Therefore, formation is an interactional and self-reflective process. It is the process by which someone grows in his or her own capabilities, finding a personal voice to answer his or her own life challenges. This person is self-reflective and has a consciously formed attitude towards others, knowing how to behave in relation with other humans, God and the world. Identity formation is all about this reflective nature of an independent person with a set of inner convictions. Values and norms have been appropriated into stable attitudes and beliefs that this person can work with. This attitude matters in the person's functioning in all kinds of situations, including public situations. Perhaps more than elsewhere, we have to show our character and the kind of person we are in the public arena. Here, we cannot hide behind others or in the safety of our family; we have to speak up and act by ourselves. Especially in *pluralistic* situations, where people are different and we feel the *otherness* of the others, we have to rely on ourselves, on the ways we have been formed.

Identity formation is of course complex. Significant others do play a crucial role here: parents, brothers and sisters, teachers, friends, people around us or heroes at a distance. Their opinions, views, values, examples and narratives matter to us. In school, we learn to view the world in a certain way, and we are educated in certain beliefs. However, it is we ourselves who decide what to do with these, on the basis of our inner considerations. It is the heart that directs the person. Therefore, we need to start deep inside, where decisions are made. We need to start with our desires, James K. Smith argued. He said that before we are social animals we are desiring animals, and I think he is right. Love or desire is a 'structural feature of being human' and it is 'what I desire, what I love, that animates my passion'.[10] Love can of course take different routes and fail in finding the right direction. Therefore, directing a person is part of the work of formation. We shape a character by *aiming this desire towards a particular end*.

We all desire some sort of human flourishing. Smith presented a picture of the good life as one that kindles a certain desire in us. The deeper level of this desire, he depicted as 'desiring the Kingdom'. How can this desire become part of our character, our choices, our identity? According to Smith, this desire can become an integral part of the fabric

---

10 James K. Smith, *Desiring the Kingdom. Worship, Worldview and Cultural Formation* (Grand Rapids: Baker Academic, 2009), 51.

of our dispositions.[11] He believes that desires can become part of our good *habits*, which we obtain by repeating certain actions and rituals, shaping them as our *second nature*. They turn our hearts, and 'our desire for the kingdom is inscribed in our dispositions and habits'.[12] Is Smith right? Is this, in essence, what identity formation is all about?

Indeed, one part our character is shaped by rituals and practices that we can repeat over and over to help ourselves in the rhythms and patterns of life. This is how a repertoire is formed. However, we need to acknowledge that training our habits has a mechanical aspect: reproducing ourselves as the same person all the time. While it is true that our imagination and desires do not have their origin in the habitual but in something deeper, in our hearts, they are conveyed to us and kindled by narratives, histories, art and music when we wonder about what we do not know and what is new to us, about differences and otherness. Our habits help us behave in the same way, react in the same way, do pattern-like things. Our desires, however, go deeper and reach farther than what our habits can make us learn. Love is more encompassing, giving us desires and insights that come unexpectedly, surprisingly, and that are bigger than what we can conjure by ourselves. It creates moments of *kairos*: a sudden insight or conviction that changes our whole mindset, feeling or belief system. Life is too complex to be approached by habit alone. I think the habitual is overestimated in the process of identity formation.

Let us examine an example to illustrate the foregoing. When we want to do good, we sometimes have to behave against what our habits tell us to do. Our habits tell us to do the normal things in a normal way. It is normal not to lend money to someone who cannot pay us back. It is normal to pay less to a person who has worked less hours than a person who has worked more hours. Yet, these are the examples of the ultimate good given in Scripture. Perhaps the priest and Levite acted more according to habit than the Good Samaritan did. We are trained not to trust strangers, but what if some unknown neighbour wants to borrow our car? The challenges of life are larger than what habits can teach us. Therefore, we need to get in touch with the ultimate good through narratives, examples, explicit commandments. Some sort of authority has to teach and show us how to choose the ultimate good. It is not our tendencies or dispositions that should guide our actions; it is our heart that needs to be convinced about what is right and that has to make the right choice.

---

11 Ibidem, 55.
12 Ibidem, 56.

I believe that habits are just one element of identity formation. They perhaps fill our desires, but not all of them, and they do not direct our desires altogether. There are thus two things that have to be dealt with in identity formation; Paul Ricoer called them *identity idem* and *identity ipse*. *Identity idem* means sameness. In some situations we always do the same, often in fixed patterns and routines. This is what habit teaches us to do, and of course they form our tendencies and shape our repertoire and self-image. *Identity ipse*, on the other hand, means showing our unique character by remaining faithful to our deepest convictions, keeping our promises to others. Do we run away from others when they need us? Are we really courageous when courage counts? These attitudes are informed by the desire to do good in situations that are beyond our control and expectation. It is in such situations that our true character shows up. These situations are most often those that are new to us. In such situations, we see who we really are in the light of our beliefs and deeper convictions.

Educating pupils in civic attitudes
Identity formation focuses on the cultivation of good habits and firm convictions. Through practice and reflection, examples and narratives, a person appropriates attitudes (moral, spiritual, cultural) that become characteristic of himself or herself. This person knows how to behave, act and judge independently and in relation to others. Social skills are developed in the same process. However, in public life, specific attitudes are required. Dutch schools are tasked to train their pupils to become active citizens, contributing to the wider community; to train their pupils to support social integration, to cope with the social and cultural differences they may encounter later in life; and to teach them democratic values. Schools have to train their pupils to participate in civic traditions. For schools, this is both a challenge and an opportunity to show that they are not just enclaves existing for their own sake, or a subculture, and that they are helping boost the dimension of socialisation. Their *particular* identity should support what is *universal*. Christian schools have to educate children to be citizens among others, respecting people's differences, being agents of social cohesion, promoting shalom for the world.

How can Christian schools do this? They can help create a shared repertoire. A repertoire consists of 'routines, words, tools, ways of doing things, stories, gestures, symbols, genres, actions or concepts'.[13] The elements can be heterogeneous but acquire coherence from 'the fact that

---
13 Wenger, *Communities of Practice*, 83.

they belong to the practice of a community pursuing an enterprise'. In our case, this community is the community of citizens in a village, neighbourhood, city and the wider political community. The repertoire 'includes the discourse by which members create meaningful statements about the world'. This meaning is not fixed, the repertoire offers 'resources for negotiating meaning'.[14] This requires perspectives on what is meaningful in the public realm. This meaning is transferred to civic attitudes and public conduct. It can be done in the classroom (and elsewhere), offering content, ideas and perspectives for a shared repertoire.

Most importantly, pupils and students must learn that civic attitudes are rooted in moral attitudes. We belong to wider communities and must learn to love others and care for them. Here, relations and social imagination come in. By these I mean images or pictures of the people and the wider community that we want to serve. Needed are stories about and ideas of what human flourishing means in such a context. It is also necessary to practice and apply love, and here, action comes in. The repertoire offers tools for these practices, but it all starts by feeding our hearts with the right desires, if not the felt obligation, to be there for the wider community and to contribute our share to good relations, social cohesion, peace and harmony. Teachers can talk about these attitudes, which can grow as part of our identity and character and can become part of our daily routines and habits.

The shared repertoire is a way of functioning and participation in society. It is not the repertoire of the school but the repertoire of the wider community, embedded in cultural patterns and customs and containing a set of values appropriate for public life. We cannot learn to participate by habit alone, and to participate by heart requires more. It is not a matter of desiring to serve others we do not know and to get acquainted with people who are different from and strange to us. To become familiar with such people, we need to become familiar with the values, concepts and ideas that help us shape our public conduct and relations with others. Acceptance, tolerance, social cohesion, integration and harmony will result from that. Christian school pupils should be educated for shalom, to pursue what is truly good: for Bavinck, love and justice, which are social virtues. For the Christian school of today, however, I would translate 'what is truly good' as three core values: solidarity, hospitality and justice. Schools need a *discourse* in these areas to *create meaningful statements about the world*. This discourse supports the shaping of civic

---

14 Ibidem.

attitudes and can have these three cardinal values as its core.

Teaching *solidarity* means teaching pupils to love all humanity. Jan Amos Comenius once called the school *humanitas officinae*, a workshop of humanity. The school serves the human world, and pupils are formed and educated for the wider community than just for the temporal community of the school. Therefore, pupils must learn to love all humanity and share their suffering and feel their pain. They need to know that they can contribute to the welfare of all, not just to that of some people or to that of only the people in their own nation or race. Solidarity expresses this holistic value. It means bringing together broken parts, creating unity out of several separate pieces. This is not necessarily a Christian value, but it cannot be realised without loving one's neighbour, as Jesus teaches us. In addition, we must not forget that Christianity stretches out to all humanity; it is universal in its scope and action.

Teaching *hospitality* means teaching pupils to serve all humanity. Hospitality entails acceptance and tolerance. We cannot open our house, receive guests, bring in resources and share what we have without accepting others and without tolerance. Hospitality is an orientation involving honouring others, expressing ourselves in acts of welcome. It is a concept with civic ramifications. The school can set examples of hospitality and can stimulate reflection on it. It is important for pupils to learn that living with others in the wider community means helping those who do not belong to their own ingroup, accepting people with opinions and ways of life different from theirs and being kind and open to such people. Hospitality helps us see the interests of others and makes us prepared and willing to open our homes and communities to them as well. The welfare of the community is our concern, so we have to be there and to support its members and share with them whatever we can. This is the deeper meaning of hospitality I am hinting at.

Teaching *justice* means teaching pupils to judge rightly. They need to form the right opinion about all kinds of situations in public life. Their judgment, wisdom and *prudentia* are important. They must be able to judge what is right or wrong to do, what is democratic or not, what serves the public interest and what does not. Through their public conduct they add meaning to the public action of the wider community. Participation is never without judgment. Thus, pupils need to be formed to be agents of justice and shalom. This is an important task of the school and is part of the *discourse* needed to help pupils develop civic attitudes.

Teaching pupils these three aforementioned values can kindle in their hearts the desire to serve the wider community. They must eventually feel it their calling to serve other humans, to be of help to others, to be hospitable and to promote the well-being of others, supported by a clear judgment about what has to be done to pursue what is good for the community. This requires social imagination, imagining how to live together in the here and now, imagining shalom, not mistrust and an apprehensive mind, as was the case in the small circle of Tara Westover. She grew up in an environment without such a social imagination of a flourishing life with others. Young people need examples to observe and practices of such a life to acquire the *repertoire* of a citizen inspired by Christian wisdom. Where do we find these examples and practices?

Civic attitudes and social practices of the Church
The civic attitudes taught in school need some sort of practice to engender the solidarity, hospitality, judgment and democratic behaviour needed in society at large. The insights of pupils should be translated into greater insight and greater tolerance, mutual understanding and compassion, for the common good and shalom. However, schools do not operate in the public realm. Pupils can observe all sorts of situations outside the school and can learn from others' practices, but what about their own activities as next-generation citizens? They carry out all kinds of minute tasks and join sports clubs and associations, among others. Some of them are idealistic, engaging in bigger endeavours such as scouting. Political parties and environmental organisations have youth departments, where youngsters can participate in certain practices and can learn to cooperate and create meaning together with others.

What about the Church? The Church is a public institution, open to everyone, caring for everyone, with a message for the entire world. The scope of the Church is universal because the scope of the Gospel is universal. In the last centuries, however, the Church was pushed back to its own domain due to the diversification of society. More recently, however, the Church has been invited even by local governments to become active in all kinds of social work, including serving as informal networks of help and care. The Church has not ceased to support faith-based organisations and schools that work for the public benefit, but in that case, it is others who do the job. Now, Churches are challenged to practice what they preach, and this means reactivating a role that has almost been forgotten by believers. The Church influences people's lifestyles and the choices that people make, and can engender Christian practices and attitudes. The Church can set examples of Christian practices and in so doing can contribute much to public life.

Let us take for example *hospitality* as a value and practice, with its public ramifications. This is the value and attitude of receiving other people as guests, opening our doors to them and sharing with them our resources. In recent years, Churches have become more open to people looking for shelter, food and practical and moral support. I know of a church that provides *buddies* for 80 lonely people. On certain Sundays, the *buddies* bring all kinds of items they think their partners need (e.g. clothes, books, furniture). Once in a while, the church offers such items for free to other people who need them. This helps the poor people in the church's neighbourhood. At other occasions, churches share food or help people get their official paperwork done. I consider these Christian practices engendering civic attitudes. Through these practices, the Church creates space for people to practice pursuit of the public interest and mutual engagement, connection and social cohesion. In so doing, the Church employs its bridging social capital.

The Church can act as the vanguard of new social practices, being a 'contrast community' (*Hauerwas*) or a 'powerstation' (Schilder), building a body larger than the Church. When schools embrace the same values, why should they not join such practices? For the new generations, this offers a fine opportunity to enhance their experience. It helps them see how compassion feeds civic attitudes such as tolerance and advocacy, bridging social gaps and differences. It helps them test their growing convictions, be supportive of others and train their preparedness and ability to help, hopefully eventually as a 'second nature'. In this way, schools can make a connection with meaningful practices of socialisation. The Church, for its part, can become more open to civil society. Reflection on hospitality can open a fresh path to do this. The Church can pour out love and justice in public life in more ways than it is perhaps aware of, and young people can be trained to be serving social animals, equipped with civic attitudes to function in the world out there.

Roel Kuiper is a professor of Christian Identity in Societal Practices at the TU Kampen.

Contributors

Trevor Cooling (1951) is Emeritus Professor of Christian Education at Canterbury Christ Church University, UK. His research interests are in Christian learning, church schools and religious education as a subject in secular schools.

Maarten Kater (1962) is Professor of Practical Theology at the Theological University of Apeldoorn, The Netherlands. His research interest is in homiletics, specifically informed by the letter to the Hebrews.

Roel Kuiper (1962) is professor Christian Identity in Societal Practices at the Theological University Kampen. He was educated as a philosopher at the Free University and published widely in the areas of social and political philosophy, Christian worldview and Christian education. In Kampen he is involved in projects with Christian schools to study and shape their identity as a school. He is member of the scientific Board of VERUS.

Ferdi Kruger (1965) is a professor of Practical Theology at the Faculty of Theology of the North-West University since 2014. He is research director for the Unit for Reformational Theology and the Development of the South African Society. He is also the author of several scholarly articles and focuses on the forming and functioning of attitudes within the research fields of Homiletics and Liturgics.

Bram de Muynck (1961) is professor of Christian Education at the Theological University of Apeldoorn and professor of education at Driestar Christian University in Gouda. His research area is Personhood formation and Identity. He published about spirituality of teachers, identity of schools and a number of topics related to formation. He is regional editor of the *International Journal of Christianity and education*.

Hans Schaeffer (1972) studied theology in Kampen, Tübingen and London, and is now professor of Practical Theology at Theological University Kampen. In 2019 he published a book on liturgy and practical ecclesiology: *Kerk om te vieren. Praktisch-theologische reflecties op kerkzijn* (Summum Academic: Kampen, 2019).

David I. Smith (1966), PhD in Curriculum Studies, University of London. Professor of Education and Director of the Kuyers institute for Christian Teaching and Learning, Calvin University, Grand Rapids, Michigan, USA. Recent books include On Christian Teaching: Practicing faith in the Classroom (Eerdmans, 2018).

Bernd Wannenwetsch (1959) is Professor of Systematic Theology and Ethics, has taught at the Universities of Oxford, Aberdeen, and currently at the Freie Theologische Hochschule Gießen.

Index

Arendt, Hannah	70, 128
Aristotle, Artisotelian	9, 57-60, 63, 64, 67, 68, 130,
attitude	10, 14, 16, 40, 49, 81, 107-126, 129-141
Au, Wayne	26
Bavinck, Herman	10, 130, 133, 138
Bible	14, 15, 20, 29, 31, 32, 33, 37, 38, 40-55, 68, 69, 78, 80, 81, 85-89, 93, 99, 105, 111, 116, 117, 124, 132
biblical authority	9, 37, 40, 43-47, 51, 53, 54, 56
biblical faithfulness	47, 53,
Bonhoeffer, Dietrich	15, 25, 29, 30, 65, 71
catechism	7, 8, 94
character	8, 58-60, 62-65, 67, 69, 75, 76, 85, 104, 118, 129, 130, 132-138
church	7-11, 13-15, 18-22, 38, 40, 54, 59, 60, 65, 67, 71, 72, 75, 77-105, 107, 109, 116, 123, 126, 127, 129-132, 140, 141
citizenship	10, 131, 133
civic education	64, 70, 127-141
cognition, cognitive	10, 15, 19, 20, 107, 109-126
confirmation ceremonials	13
constructivism	40, 43-45, 50, 54
critical realism	48-50
Crombrugge, Hans van	18, 22
curriculum	9, 10, 20, 25, 26, 35, 78, 80, 85
cultural mandate	10, 132, 133
disputation	105
doctrine	10, 15, 93, 95, 96, 98, 99, 102
doxology	96, 97, 105
ecclesia 7	59, 65, 67, 75, 76, 81, 83, 84, 88, 91, 92, 99, 103-105
education	7-10, 13-17, 19, 20, 22, 24-26, 28-31, 35, 37-44, 46-48, 51, 54, 57-59, 70, 75-78, 80, 82-91, 94, 95, 101, 102, 105, 107-115, 121-123, 125-131, 133, 134

education, christian (religious)	15, 17, 24, 35, 39, 42, 43, 48, 54, 76, 91, 129, 134
education, theological	9, 10, 24, 75, 77, 78, 80, 82-90, 105, 107, 109, 112, 122, 125, 126
education, transformative	10, 107, 108, 110, 122, 126
educator, *see: teacher*	
ethics	54, 58-60, 63-66, 85, 90, 92, 102, 118
faith and learning	24, 31, 33, 76
Farron, Tim	37-41, 45-47, 55, 56
formation	7-11, 13-29, 31, 33, 35, 36, 57-60, 62-70, 72, 74-83, 85-89, 91-95, 98, 101-104, 107-109, 111-126, 129-137,
formation, cultural	11, 24, 77, 129, 135
formation, faith	8, 9, 14, 21, 24-27, 29, 31, 33, 35, 36, 103
formation, moral	8, 131, 133
formation, self	13, 17, 22
formation, spiritual	8, 9, 24, 35, 78, 79, 81, 87, 88, 92
formational climate	18, 19
formational context	18
formational intervention	18, 20
Hauerwas, Stanley	29, 59, 60, 63, 64, 90, 92, 141
Hebrews	10, 93-95, 99-102, 104-107, 109, 110, 113, 116-122
hermeneutical space	17
hermeneutics	46, 50-53, 55, 56, 87, 89, 102, 115
Hull, John	40-42, 46
inner speech	110, 114, 115, 118
Jennings, Willie James	79, 80
Kohnstamm, Philip Abraham	13, 17, 22
Kuyper, Abraham	23, 85
learning environment	9, 28, 31, 35, 91, 114, 124
lex audiendi	101, 102, 106
lex credendi	10, 91, 93-95, 98-106
lex orandi	10, 91, 93-106
lex vivendi	102, 106
liturgy/liturgical	10, 20, 75, 77, 79, 87-106, 112, 117, 119, 122-125
McGrath, Alister	46, 49, 50

MacIntyre, Alisdair,	57, 59, 63
meditation	105
ministry	10, 24, 75-79, 81, 83-92, 103, 106, 107, 123
Palmer, Parker J.	35
parents	13, 14, 16-19, 21, 60, 62-64, 70, 72, 127, 135
Paul (apostle)	7, 57, 60, 66, 72, 73, 98, 121
Piaget	10, 110, 113, 114, 118
pedagogy	16, 20, 25, 29, 30, 31, 33, 36, 42, 51, 66, 76, 86-88, 108
pedagogical design	9, 23, 25, 31, 35
perceptions	107, 110-112, 115, 118, 124-126
Pollefeyt, Didier	17, 18
polis	9, 59, 62-64, 68, 70
practice/practices	9, 10, 22, 24-31, 33-35, 57, 59, 61, 62, 72, 76-86, 88-94, 96-99, 101-103, 105, 106, 110-113, 127-129, 131-133, 136-138, 140, 141
pre-understanding	52
psalms	9, 61, 62, 64, 66, 69, 70
reflection, theological	9, 78-85, 90-92, 95, 97, 125
responsibility	9, 17, 18, 35, 39, 41, 79, 108, 119, 128, 131
schemes	59, 72, 86, 110, 114
Smith, James K.A.	10, 20, 24, 33, 76, 77, 79, 88, 135, 136
social media	13, 18
teachers	8-11, 13, 14, 16-21, 25, 33-47, 49, 51, 54-56, 76, 115, 117, 121, 123, 131, 134, 135, 138
theology	7, 9, 10, 16, 22, 25, 27, 28, 38, 41, 46, 49, 50, 54, 59, 78-91, 93-109, 116, 122, 123, 125
torah	9, 62-64, 68, 70
tradition	15, 24, 25, 40, 46, 58, 61, 62, 64, 67, 75, 79, 82, 83, 85, 87, 88, 90, 109, 128, 137
traditioning	9, 57, 60-64, 66-68, 70-74, 87
transform/transformation/ transformative	10, 57, 66, 80, 87, 89, 92, 107, 108, 110, 117, 119, 120, 122-126
virtue	9, 33, 47, 58-60, 63-65, 69, 71, 76, 77, 104, 128, 130-132, 138
Vygotsky	10, 110, 113-115, 118
Wright, Christopher,	47, 51, 53
Wright, N.T.	46, 48, 53-55
youth work	7, 8, 13, 16-19, 21